KV-325-183

York St John University
3 8025 00632534 7

THE ACADEMIC CAESAR

In 1976 SAGE published a series of short 'university papers', which led to the publication of the QASS series (or the 'little green books' as they became known to researchers). Almost 40 years since the release of the first 'little green book', SAGE is delighted to offer a new series of swift, short and topical pieces in the ever-growing digital environment.

SAGE *Swifts* offer authors a new channel for academic research with the freedom to deliver work outside the conventional length of journal articles. The series aims to give authors speedy access to academic audiences through digital first publication, space to explore ideas thoroughly, yet at a length which can be readily digested, and the quality stamp and reassurance of peer-review.

THE ACADEMIC CAESAR

UNIVERSITY LEADERSHIP IS HARD

STEVE FULLER

Los Angeles | London | New Delhi
Singapore | Washington DC | Melbourne

Los Angeles | London | New Delhi
Singapore | Washington DC | Melbourne

SAGE Publications Ltd
1 Oliver's Yard
55 City Road
London EC1Y 1SP

SAGE Publications Inc.
2455 Teller Road
Thousand Oaks, California 91320

SAGE Publications India Pvt Ltd
B 1/I 1 Mohan Cooperative Industrial Area
Mathura Road
New Delhi 110 044

SAGE Publications Asia-Pacific Pte Ltd
3 Church Street
#10-04 Samsung Hub
Singapore 049483

Editor: Natalie Aguilera
Editorial assistant: Delayna Spencer
Production editor: Vanessa Harwood
Marketing manager: Sally Ransom
Cover design: Jen Crisp
Typeset by: C&M Digitals (P) Ltd, Chennai, India
Printed and bound by CPI Group (UK) Ltd,
Croydon, CR0 4YY

First published 2016

Library of Congress Control Number: 2016944804

British Library Cataloguing in Publication data

A catalogue record for this book is available from the British Library

ISBN 978-1-4739-6178-4
eISBN 978-1-4739-8491-2

CONTENTS

ABOUT THE AUTHOR

Steve Fuller is Auguste Comte Professor of Social Epistemology in the Department of Sociology at the University of Warwick, UK. Originally trained in history and philosophy of science, he is the author of more than 20 books. In recent years, his work has focused on the future of the intellectual life as well as the future of humanity more generally, which he calls 'Humanity 2.0'.

ACKNOWLEDGEMENTS

Many people have spurred me – directly and indirectly – to write this book, which is about academic leadership at the start of the 21st century, taking both the past and the future perhaps a bit more seriously than current preoccupations would allow. These people include Thomas Basbøll (who brings out my inner Ezra Pound), Kean Birch, Rebecca Boden, Craig Calhoun, Mark Carrigan, Jim Collier, Robert Frodeman, Davydd Greenwood, Reiner Grundmann, Greg Hearn, Britt Holbrook, Jonathan Imber, David Rooney, Roger Sugden, Wu Wei, Emilie Whitaker, James Wilsdon and Susan Wright. The book is dedicated to my long-time friend, the radical institutionalist economist Philip Mirowski. About ten years ago, he pulled me aside after a talk I had given at the University of Ghent and warned me against highlighting the rent-seeking character of academic knowledge production, as that was a gift to the Robespierre-like epistemic horizons of neo-liberalism. Mirowski (2013) went on to develop this warning into a full-blown jeremiad about neo-liberalism, but I have always had a soft spot for Nietzsche's Zarathustra: 'What doesn't kill me makes me stronger'.

INTRODUCTION: THE NEO-LIBERAL MOMENT IN HIGHER EDUCATION AND THE NEED FOR AN ACADEMIC CAESAR

1 MY OWN QUEST TO FIGURE OUT WHAT'S WORTH DEFENDING IN ACADEMIA

I always try to be ahead of the curve: I like to know our current position and then think how we should proceed to reach a desirable future. This assumes a general direction to history, which nevertheless remains open to the future and hence pliable to any of a number of ends and susceptible to any number of outcomes. It also means that my projections change as the data points defining the curve change. Consider it a 21st century update of John Maynard Keynes' offhand remark that when the facts change, so does his mind. At the very least, this book should make it clear that the 'university' as an idea will need to be reinvented if the assorted people, buildings and car parks that constitute 'universities' are likely to continue to perform their current functions in the coming years. We do not live in a time especially friendly to the idea of the university, and so it will require a champion, the *Academic Caesar*. But before this figure can be unveiled, the stage needs to be set. It is *the neo-liberal moment*. What follows is my thinking through this moment, which I do more sympathetically than those who normally claim to defend the university these days.

Let me start with a general point about criticism. The capacity to realize an idea such as 'the university' in a hostile environment is quite different from blaming the world when it fails to live up to its promises. Unfortunately the latter is too often what passes for 'critique' these days, something which Freud dismissed as an infantile neurosis – before he had heard of the Frankfurt School but had already heard of socialism. Critique can turn into a cure worse than its disease when pursued as an end in itself, which is to say, without any clear commitment to a feasible positive end. In that case, it fails to be the second

moment of a purposeful dialectic, which is what critique was meant to be. It is worth recalling that in the Enlightenment, critics were irksome, first in art and then in politics, precisely because they suggested how an idea could have been better realized. They were the backseat drivers and Monday morning quarterbacks of their day. They dared to replay history to demonstrate an improved result. They did not dwell on factors beyond the artist's control that would point to inevitable failure, no matter what he or she had done. Equally, they did not mourn missed political opportunities that will never return. Unfortunately, today's self-appointed 'critics' strike just these more fatalistic poses, not least with regard to the future of the university.

I have been casting a critical eye on the future of academia ever since I started the interdisciplinary field of 'social epistemology' thirty years ago, mainly because the university is the only institution expressly dedicated to producing knowledge as a public good. I shall regularly return to this point. However, as the political economy of higher education has changed, so too has my perspective. Until the early years of the post-Cold War era (say, up to 1995), I was focused on the tendency for disciplinary structures in universities to impede intellectual innovation and obscure public access to knowledge. As I used to put it: Disciplines are 'necessary evils' – the more necessary, the more evil. Thus, I have consistently been a champion of interdisciplinarity who has tried to lead by example (e.g. Fuller 1988, Fuller and Collier 2004). It helps to explain my efforts to overcome the legacy of Thomas Kuhn, whose standing as the most influential theorist of science of the second half of the 20th century – based on Kuhn (1970) – rested on a celebration of 'paradigms', his name for discipline-based inquiry (e.g. Fuller 2000b, Fuller 2003). As we shall see in Chapter 2, this vision remains alive and well in peer review, about which I also have serious reservations. My opposition to this general 'Kuhnification' of academic life also helps to explain my rather positive disposition towards 'intellectuals', understood as inquirers who do not see academic inquiry as an end in itself but a means to greater public Enlightenment (Fuller 2005, Fuller 2009).

However, the terms of engagement were decisively altered with the advent of 'mode 2 knowledge production', a piece of Euro-jargon that became popular in the wake of Gibbons et al. (1994). It marked the morphing of social democratic sensibilities about the need for knowledge to be 'relevant' and 'accountable' into the neo-liberal standards that are in effect today. What changed with the end of the Cold War was the state's role in knowledge production, as it became less directly involved in the nation's capital development and social security. This is often described as the 'decline of the state'. But the description does not quite do justice to what has happened. After all, the state remains very active, but largely in the creation and regulation of markets, whereby private producers compete to do things that in the past the state would have done under its own authority and with its own resources. Yet, the state remains very much a client – often the principal one – for what these markets produce, as it continues to shop on behalf of the public good.

I first unveiled the concept of 'Academic Caesar' at a UNESCO conference on the future of higher education in Paris in December 2004 (Fuller 2006c). The presentation included a chart, which I had been already using for five years to represent the choppy waters in which an aspiring Academic Caesar would need to navigate to maintain the university's autonomy in the face of neo-liberalization (cf. Fuller 2001). The chart appears here as Figure 1, which aims to translate the 'Modespeak' introduced in Gibbons et al. (1994) between its

MODESPEAK	NOT THIS...	BUT THAT...
'Codified/Tacit Knowledge' (Conversion Principle)	Performance/Competence (Creativity)	Fixed/Variable Capital (Knowledge Management)
'Context of Application'	Applied Research	Client-Centred Research
'Globalization'	Universalization	Specialization
'Heterogeneity'	Anti-Homogeneity	Anti-Autonomy
'Hybrid Agora/Forum' (University Redefined)	Knowledge Unifier	Knowledge Advertiser
'Informatization of Society'	Knowledge Mediates Social Relations	Knowledge Alienated from Individuals
'Knowledge Industries'	University Privileged	University De-Privileged
'Massification of Higher Education'	Knowledge Adds Value	Knowledge Devalued
'Pluralization of Elites'	Knowledge Workers Respected	Knowledge Workers Modularized
'Reflexivity'	Critical of Context	Adaptive to Context
'Social Capital'	Public Good	Corporate Property
'Social Distribution of Knowledge'	Integrated Unit (Institution)	Dispersed Network (Interaction)
'Socially Robust Knowledge'	Universally Resilient Knowledge (Science)	Locally Plastic Knowledge (Culture)
'Technology Transfer'	Academia Legitimates Industry (19th century)	Academia Services Industry (21st century)
'Transdisciplinarity'	Interdisciplinarity	Antidisciplinarity

Figure 1 'MODESPEAK': KNOWLEDGE SOCIETY NEWSPEAK

social democratic ('not this…') and neo-liberal ('but that…') guises. That the move between these two guises has been relatively seamless reflects the fact that it has been often made by the same people.

In one sense, neo-liberalism could have been anticipated – namely, if one considers the historical trajectory of economics' relationship to the concept of value. As soon as the locus of economic value began to shift from labour to utility in the third quarter of the 19th century, the balance of power began to move from the producer to the consumer of goods, ultimately including knowledge itself. At that point, the holders of power began to shift from those who could collectivize production (e.g. unionization) to those who could collectivize consumption (e.g. public relations). To be sure, a good century passed before the full effects of this conceptual shift were fully realized in academia, since the old producer-based notion of value has lingered for quite a long time, especially in nostalgic understandings of 'science as a vocation', to recall Max Weber's (1958) famous formulation.

To see what I mean, consider 'labour–management' conflicts, which were so central to 20th-century industrial policy and survive residually today. In such conflicts, 'labour' collectivizes those performing the same role at different sites, while 'management' collectivizes those who perform different roles but work together in the same site. Unsurprisingly, then, corporatism (which took the management side) was an effective stopgap against more radical forms of socialism (which took the labour side) in the 20th century. In any case, both sides agreed that producers drive the economy but disagreed on the best way to organize production. Indeed, the last bastions of this form of economic conflict are the professions – including academia – whose guild-like character harks back to the original source of labour's valorization. I refer to the medieval guilds, whose legal protections were gradually extended to include all workers in the 19th century – if only in principle. The historic benchmark for academic self-understanding in these terms was the union-like American Association of University Professors, which was founded by John Dewey and other Progressives in 1915 as a foil to imperious university presidents and boards of trustees.

What economists declare as their 'marginal revolution' of the 1870s marked the beginning of the shift in thinking about capitalism from the producer's to the consumer's standpoint. Whereas the former stressed the world of scarcity that resulted in diminishing returns on investment in factors of production (e.g. the degradation of land through overuse), the latter stressed the world of abundance potentially provided by diminishing marginal utility, namely, that people derive less satisfaction with each additional unit consumed and thus are ripe to be driven to consume elsewhere. It led to an increasing capitalist focus on the marketing *vis-à-vis* the production of goods in the 20th century, which was facilitated by greater efficiencies on the production side. This is the trajectory that leads to a reliance on 'Mad Men' to grow the economy by manufacturing new consumer demand which can only be met by new goods – even if only marginally different from the old ones. The fullest realization of this ideal is, of course, Apple, whose founder Steve Jobs cast himself as the ideal user of its computer products rather than its genius inventor. He succeeded by fostering an enormous 'community' of users who would follow his lead in being wowed by whatever minuscule improvement he unveiled. The pushback from this strategy – that is, the equivalent of strikes and other labour–management conflicts of yore – appears as consumer revolts mounted on the 'value for money' principle.

An aspiring Academic Caesar could turn the above paradigm shift in value orientation to his or her own purposes most 'easily' – in both its positive and negative senses – by gravitating towards the policy of 'lifelong learning'. This is the idea that whatever advantage a university degree may give you in getting your first job, it is unlikely to serve you through your entire working life. This is not because the original degree was useless; rather, its utility was predicated on an expiration date, one dictated not only by normal market conditions but also by innovations that (presumably) the university is best positioned to capture for the public good. Thus, your initial tuition fees, albeit high, allow you entry into a world that will look after your epistemic needs in every possible and increasingly sensitive way. This is a deeper commitment than US-style alumni and alumnae, who are presumed to have left 'alma mater' ('nurturing mother' in Latin) to pursue autonomous lives. To be sure, they are invited back, but more in the spirit of shareholders than dependants. In contrast, 'lifelong learning' is a more Jobsian proposition that would keep the umbilical cord between the alma mater and its matriculants intact forever, alerting them regularly when they need to refresh their credentials ('upgrade') in mini-courses, etc. Of course, this strategy could prove a challenge for universities not so close to the cutting edge of innovation at a particular time.

In any case, the implications of the state's neo-liberal turn are quite profound for universities. Throughout most of the modern period – and especially with the rise of the welfare state – the university has enjoyed various monopoly privileges as a knowledge producer. This is a tripartite legacy, drawing on the leading European cultures of the modern period – German, English and French – each exemplified by a major 19th-century figure.

Pride of place belongs to the visionary Prussian minister of education, Wilhelm von Humboldt (1767–1835), who persuaded successive generations of policymakers – as well as the general public – that academia's distinctive dedication to both research and teaching was crucial to any long-term nation-building strategy. In today's neo-liberal terms, universities replenish the stock of human capital for each new cohort by making the latest thinking generally available. The next figure of note is Master of Trinity College, Cambridge, William Whewell (1794–1866), who argued that while in principle anyone might make inventions or discoveries, only academics can certify them as proper knowledge and their makers as truly knowledgeable in what they have made. Thus, Whewell ensured that the university kept ahead of the Industrial Revolution by incorporating the natural sciences in ways that made them the progressive face of the university in the 20th century – not least through his coinage of 'scientist' to name an academically credentialed profession. Finally, Auguste Comte (1798–1857), the founder of positivism, was responsible for the narrative sensibility that underwrites the university's continued centrality to societal progress, even though he himself was a cultish outsider, comparable in social status to, say, Ayn Rand. Comte rewrote the Enlightenment history of human progress in terms of discipline-based stages, with theology and philosophy eventually yielding to empirically based sciences, whose increasing complexity culminates in 'sociology', understood as the science of policymaking. And even if the discipline nowadays called 'sociology' is not necessarily the relevant vehicle, the Comtean presumption remains insofar as societal value continues to be invested in discipline-based 'expertise'.

Whatever else neo-liberalism does, it challenges this tripartite claim for academic privilege by recasting the university as comparable to a landowner who takes advantage of scarcity in the market to extract much higher rents from tenants than are needed to maintain the land's value – say, by forcing students to undergo tuition that is only marginally connected to their future source of income (McKenzie and Tullock 2012: Part V). I shall return to this charge periodically, since it is quite serious and not entirely unfounded. Suffice it to say, the effect of this recasting has been to shift the onus on to universities to justify their existence.

When one considers the massive public and, increasingly, private resources dedicated to funding universities, and the fact that both teaching and research at advanced levels can be – and have been – done more efficiently outside universities, the social function of universities can no longer be taken for granted. Indeed, just in time for the start of the 2015–16 academic year, the UK branch of one of the world's leading accounting firms, Ernst & Young, announced that it would no longer require a university degree as a condition of employment. Instead it would administer its own tests to prospective junior employees.

This may turn out to be a tipping point towards the end of the university as an all-purpose credentials mill that feeds the 'knowledge-based' economy. While university heads have long complained that it is demeaning to reduce academic value to a labour market signal – 'a good degree = a good job prospect' – perhaps even the economists have been too generous. To be sure, Silicon Valley and its emulators have long administered their own in-house tests to job candidates, but Ernst & Young, a large and established international employer, has now followed suit.

Given the rapid advance of neo-liberalism, I have increasingly focused on defending the uniqueness of the university as a corporate form. Academics, though robust in defending their personal rights to free inquiry, have been generally both slow and poor at defending their institutional home (Fuller 2009: chap. 3). Indeed, academics tend to be either hostile or indifferent not only to university management but also to the more general intellectual culture (aka 'the media'), all of which are portrayed as distorting various features of the academic mission, which in practice is best correlated with the academic being allowed to do as he or she wishes. All told, academics are not the most sympathetic or perhaps even the most socially reflexive people one might wish them to be. It is clear that the university will need a champion who perseveres not merely with but often in spite of academics. At the same time, this Academic Caesar will also need to acquire some of the functions of the state – especially at the regulatory level – that the state itself has divested to the marketplace.

My thinking about the need for an Academic Caesar was prompted by *Fortune* magazine editor Thomas Stewart's (1997) characterization of the university as a 'dumb organization', in contrast to a fast-food chain like McDonald's, which is his paradigm case of a 'smart organization'. Put crudely, the former is a dumb whole that nevertheless consists of individually smart parts and the latter a smart whole that is managed to emerge from its individually dumb parts. Stewart himself was making an argument for the specific expertise of those who can manage the knowledge flows in an organization, which was becoming known as 'knowledge management' in business circles (Fuller 2002). In this context, normal academic administration constitutes bad management practice because the talent is simply allowed to do whatever it wants and so the overall product is in many cases *less* than the sum of its producers. One indicator of this might be a university that houses many brilliant academics but no one associates their brilliance with their being at that university. By that standard, Stewart would have to count Harvard and Oxford as well managed because rarely do the achievements of its academics outshine the sheer fact that the academics are housed there. Even the business world might learn from these two venerable institutions about how to protect and promote the corporate brand.

The usual knowledge management response to the university's organizational dumbness is to dismember the Humboldtian settlement by disaggregating the processes of research and teaching, which effectively commodifies their respective products as patents and credentials. This move is understood against the larger neo-liberal backdrop in which the university is no longer the monopoly provider of knowledge as a public good, but rather a public-private partnership playing in multiple markets, in which rival providers (e.g. corporate-sponsored research parks and digital diploma mills) are often offering more attractive prices for more customized products. The US institutionalist economist Philip Mirowski (2010) has observed that this development tracks Alfred Chandler's (1962) history of the modern corporation, which shares the same medieval collegial roots as universities and also underwent something similar to Humboldt's integrationist moment in the 19th century, before ending up in today's scaled-up and wide-scoped 'multi-divisional firm', which corresponds to what Clark Kerr (1963) memorably dubbed the 'multiversity'.

However, Chandler's corporate history does not end happily. Starting in the 1980s, shareholders became sceptical about the viability of large complex firms competing in multiple fluctuating markets. It has led to a massive divestment of corporate assets, not least the R&D divisions that had been the source of much high-tech scientific innovation in the 20th century. Indeed, many if not most corporate functions are now subcontracted and outsourced – typically to academics, abetted by university administrators who in their quest to demonstrate their economic relevance to policymakers make few demands on business to ensure that their own institutions do not become similarly hollowed out. We live with the consequences of this lack of foresight, as the academic staff of most large universities are now on (sometimes renewable) short-term contracts. Little surprise, then, that they have as little commitment to the future of their employer as it has to them; hence, the need for an Academic Caesar to provide a direction forward.

2 COMPETING CONCEPTIONS OF UNIVERSITY GOVERNANCE: ACADEMIC CAESARISM AND NEO-LIBERALISM

The United States is both impressive and anomalous when it comes to understanding the state of academia past, present and future. It has been the undisputed world leader since the end of the Second World War, and some might argue since the end of the First World War. Its academic system has always been large and diverse, yet the federal government has played a relatively minor role in this success – except during the Cold War, when in many instances it was the dominant player. Nevertheless, the US to this day lacks any ministry for education and/or research with the power to set national policy on the allocation of resources or the prioritizing of objectives. This is not to deny that government officials have made many hortatory statements along these lines, but their capacity for enforcing their will is largely indirect, requiring the support of courts, state legislatures, etc. In effect, this has meant that the federal government's biggest influence on higher education and research policy has been at the gross level of providing or withdrawing material resources, as in the case of the 1862 Morrill Act, which released state-owned property to allow for the creation of 'land-grant' universities.

In contrast, in the world's second leading academic power, the United Kingdom, the central government has a stronger policymaking hand. This position of power has also been characteristic of nations that have aspired and succeeded at improving the lot of their people. Moreover, with its combination of a strong democratic culture and a profoundly liberal sensibility, the UK has become *de facto* the world's testing ground for adventurous policies in education and research, many of which have been copied and adapted, with varying degrees of success. In this respect, the UK has been 'always already' neo-liberal. To be sure, many readers will bristle at this point. But consider the universally lauded 'Robbins Report' (Robbins 1963), which licensed the creation of several campus-based, social science-friendly universities, including Essex, Sussex, Lancaster, York and my own, Warwick – all of which have recently celebrated their fiftieth anniversaries at the top of the world league tables for universities of their vintage. The report is understood in the UK as a high watermark for the recognition of the value of higher education to society at large.

The report's author, Lionel Robbins (1898–1984), chaired the economics department at the London School of Economics (LSE) in its most formative period, the 1930s, when he hired Friedrich Hayek, who had become Margaret Thatcher's favourite economist by the time he died. Yet, like the LSE's founders, Robbins began life as a Fabian socialist, the sort of 'gradualist' whom Marxists have routinely derided as 'technocrats' and 'state capitalists', but whose ideals were slowly but surely realized in the meritocratic spirit and social engineering mentality that has generally characterized UK Labour Party policy in the 20th century, not least in the Blair–Brown years of 'New Labour'. In the future, New Labour will be seen as having governed in the spirit of William Beveridge and the post-war founders of the UK welfare state, and even Thatcher's notorious 'There is no such thing as society' will be understood as having denied *merely* the Durkheimian thesis that society has its own *sui generis* moral character, whose maintenance is entrusted to the state, but not the more basic idea that the state has a responsibility to ensure the widest range of opportunities for its citizens' advancement. Robbins himself increasingly embraced neo-classical economics' fixation on the market as the prototype for all of social life, allowing his early Fabianism to morph into a prototype for latter-day neo-liberalism. In any case, the 'socialism' of 'Fabian socialism' should be understood as referring primarily to the collective focus of state action and its responsiveness to feedback (understood perhaps in the manner of a cybernetic system) rather than to any presumptive set of normative outcomes.

However, there is no doubt that Fabianism was 'progressive', even though it lacked an agreed worked-out utopia. The Fabians took the very separation of 'means' and 'ends' in the conduct of human affairs – what is often demoted, if not demonized, as 'instrumental rationality' – as a bellwether of progress. Specifically, a society makes progress as it becomes easier for its members to disentangle means from ends, such that more paths are made available to get to more destinations. Of course, there are limits to the realization of this aspiration in any given society, but this is why the state itself needs to be actively involved in capital development to enlarge the pool of resources.

Thus, as head of the LSE's economics department, Robbins opposed the ideologically 'welfarist' tendency then dominant at Cambridge and associated with Keynes – but he did not question state intervention *per se*. Rather, he questioned specifically the insinuation of prescribed values under the rubric of 'welfare' (Proctor 1991: chap. 13). Robbins was in favour of increasing access to higher education to previously marginalized sectors of society as well as increasing the choice of universities at their disposal. However, he did not believe that a dynamic and progressive society was served by everyone aspiring to the common standard of achievement implied by 'welfare'. A good indicator of the sort of value pluralism that Robbins embraced is that his report's research assistant, Richard Layard (2005), has made a career from developing 'happiness' metrics, which relativize the concept of welfare to a sense of individual well-being independent of wealth redistribution considerations.

From where Robbins sat in the early 1960s, UK higher education still seemed to be dominated by Oxford and Cambridge, whose graduates mostly staffed all the other universities. This gave the impression that students, regardless of background or need, were being indoctrinated in elite values, with which the humanities were then most clearly associated. However, Robbins did not wish classical humanistic values to be replaced wholesale by the sort of technocratic values that he detected emerging in the welfare state. His solution to this quandary was simply to turn higher education into a market, allowing greater student choice to dilute the influence of elites and enable other disciplines, perspectives and concerns to flourish.

In short, the Robbins Report was very much grounded in market-based thinking. It aimed to break up an effective higher education monopoly and encourage trade that would be more directly responsive to spontaneous demand. In this case the trade pertained to knowledge rather than ordinary goods and services. While the demand for higher education may be spontaneous, the size and shape of the markets supplying it are not. Here markets themselves perform an educative role, a function that first made them attractive in the late 18th century, when Adam Smith and the Marquis de Condorcet promoted markets as the secret to national prosperity (Rothschild 2001). Back then 'marketization' was seen as an innovative form of state action that forced society to raise its collective game, as consumers had to become more discriminating in response to a sudden proliferation of producers (Fuller 2006a). Over time this has meant, for better or worse, a transfer of power from producers to consumers.

In the UK this has meant that the state has withdrawn fixed funding from universities, causing them to set fairly steep tuition fees. However, the state then offers students a relatively generous, low-interest loan targeted to university selection that is repayable only once their postgraduate income reaches a certain level. In this way, the state becomes the ultimate human capital investor, taking calculated risks on two fronts. On the one hand, it counts on universities repackaging themselves to attract students; on the other, on prospective students selecting wisely from among the offerings. The logic of the market dictates that collective learning occurs through trial-and-error in which everyone benefits from the mistakes of the relatively few. This is the world in which we increasingly live. The Robbins Report can be credited – or blamed – for having set it in motion.

Nowadays UK state-based provision for universities falls under the Department for Business, Innovation and Skills. This cabinet-level office is normally seen as a product of 'New Labour', in which the top minister Peter Mandelson promoted the idea, largely supported in academic circles, that universities are the engine of the impending 'knowledge economy' – the fount of job creation, domestic prosperity, competitive advantage, global esteem, etc. This was a Faustian bargain, if not a poisoned chalice – at least for those who believed that taking the additional money would entail a straightforward extension of academia's classic Humboldtian mission. Indeed, what UK academics regularly criticize as their sector's 'audit culture' derives from this agreed understanding of the university's centrality to the knowledge economy (Power 1997). Perhaps the most undesirable unintended consequence of this arrangement has been that education ('skills') and research ('innovation') are treated as separate items on the state's balance sheet, which are evaluated not only independently of each other but also potentially in terms of markets which include non-university players who specialize in one but not the other function. (Here one need only compare the most recent reports on higher education and research: Javid 2015, Nurse 2015.) Thus, the ultimate victim of the state's munificence may be the university's corporate integrity.

University administrators are reminded of the corporate integrity of their institutions whenever they make academic hiring decisions. Academics do not simply teach and do research. They are teacher-researchers. If the value added by nurturing this complex role is not already at the forefront of the state's thinking about the criteria used to fund universities, then it should certainly focus the Academic Caesar's mind. After all, even advanced technical training can be provided more efficiently outside a university. There are also more efficient places to work to produce innovative research than a university. Nevertheless, the corporate integrity of the university rests on the idea that teaching and research should be conducted if not by the same people, then at least by people in regular contact with each other. It follows that the value added by universities to society should be judged by the difference that this idea makes to the quality of the training and research provided. Such are the preferred terms of engagement between the Academic Caesar and today's neo-liberal administrator. At this point, it might be useful to contrast the provenance of the Academic Caesar and the 'neo-liberal administrator'.

The Academic Caesar is the champion of the 'Humboldtian university', an entity that needs to be understood in its original political-economic context. As Prussian education minister, Humboldt's ambition was to use the universities to produce people who by their example could constitute a strong modern state, which in 1810 was more an aspiration than a reality in Germany. Back then, Germany was a loose collection of monarchies desperate to make a mark on the world stage, all the while being forced to play catch-up with the political and economic innovations coming from France and Britain. Against this backdrop, the cultivation of *Kultur* served as a policy of epistemic self-protection – in the spirit of economic tariffs to protect native industries – but also an assertion of self-identity (Fuller 2007a: 203–7).

Thus, the Humboldtian academic was a heroic figure who led by example, a model of the free citizen at the height of his powers. This hero was originally a 'he' but it could easily be a 'she' today. Her classroom performance would inspire a questing spirit in students as they tried to bring together the disparate, often inchoate elements of their field into a coherent whole that pointed the way forward. It would matter less the ultimate validity of any such synthesis than the turn of mind that the performance represented one which remained 'never at rest', to recall the title of the standard biography of Isaac Newton (Westfall 1980). In retrospect, it is easy to see this strategy as having been very effective in branding 'Germany' in the 19th and at least the first half of the 20th century – that is, until the rise of Nazism. Thus, Germany was seen as a country whose people operated with very broad horizons and very deep concerns, ever striving in its own distinctive way, an extended sense of *Sonderweg*. Even today it is difficult to imagine, say, Martin Heidegger as having been anything other than German.

In contrast, as our discussion of the Robbins Report already suggests, neo-liberalism takes for granted a state that is neither infallible nor omnipotent, yet one that is already invested with considerable knowledge and power. In particular, the state acknowledges that beyond an informed commitment to such very broad societal ideals as liberty and progress, there remains considerable scope for their implementation. Here, the market serves as a testing ground to try out various policies for their efficacy. This approach may seem a bit odd because academics nowadays tend to think of the research and the policy environments as not only different but also consecutively related. However, common to the Fabian socialists and their neo-liberal offspring is a belief that the fundamental principles of the human condition are more-or-less established, with the differences between, say, Marx, Mill and Spencer seen as matters of emphasis, or even spin. In that case, empirical research should be about the uptake and feedback from the application of such principles in practice. This is how to understand the distinctiveness of the London School of Economics as an academic institution. The Fabians established the LSE specifically for teaching and researching into statecraft (aka 'social science'). By the time of the LSE's founding in 1895, the UK already had a highly developed civil service and its global reach was arguably at its peak, leading many to speak of a 'Pax Britannica'. However, it was not clear that the typical Oxbridge-trained humanist had the right skill-set for this complex world of global governance, which is nowadays too dismissively glossed as 'imperialism'. Against this backdrop, the LSE created its own international market for breeding forward-looking state policymakers.

The history of American higher education stands in an interesting relation to these two European models. There has always been a strong 'Humboldtian' element to this history, but less because of any specific German influence (despite the influx of German peoples to the American colonies) than that the early colleges were indeed 'cradles of liberty' in a period when the American settlers were struggling to define themselves in relation to a Europe whose interests were quickly diverging from – and often in opposition to – their own. The settlers were especially sensitive on this score because most had been forced to leave their ancestral homes due to the religious intolerance that came with the emergence of strong European national identities. Against this backdrop, the church-based foundations of the 'Ivy League' universities provided the first legally recognized corporate structures in which the cultivation of free inquiry operated as a reliable incubator for self-governing individuals, who – should the opportunity arise – might scale up their academic activities into a full-blown republican democracy of nation-wide import. It was in this spirit that Benjamin Franklin and Thomas Jefferson considered the founding of universities to have been among their most lasting achievements. This backstory needs to be kept in mind even when judging the nowadays much-derided 'fraternities', which were very active on American campuses during the War of Independence. Even more remarkable than the Ivy League's ability to lodge themselves quite consistently in the front rank of global universities over the past century is that their 'Humboldtian' blueprint did not require Humboldt at all. Harvard, Yale, Princeton, Columbia and Penn were already in existence by the mid-18th century, two generations before Humboldt launched the University of Berlin.

For the American equivalent of the Fabian/neo-liberal approach to higher education, we must turn to the gradual incorporation of academic intellectuals into government advisory roles in the Progressive Era of the early 20th century (Hofstadter 1955: chap. 4 ff). Starting with former Princeton President Woodrow Wilson, it moved to Franklin Roosevelt's 'Brain Trust' of economists and lawyers who drafted New Deal legislation, eventuating in the sociologists and psychologists that Lyndon Johnson brought in to implement the 'Great Society', the title of a book by one of the LSE's original politics lecturers, Graham Wallas (1914), who wrote it to introduce Fabian ideas to Harvard students in 1910. Thus, the half-century Progressive-Fabian link had been brought full circle. The person who best embodied that link in his career was also the most influential American journalist of the 20th century, Walter Lippmann, an advisor to every president from Wilson to Nixon. He had been one of those Harvard students addressed by Wallas, who in turn dedicated *The Great Society* to the 25-year-old Lippmann.

Wallas and Lippmann are both nowadays associated with an 'irrationalist' view of human nature, yet it would be truer to their detached, academic perspective on politics to say that they believed that current 'trends' were at best indirect measures of the sustaining underlying forces that drive human affairs. Whereas trends may be captured in statistics, these deeper causes require a kind of intellectual intuition, which is the product of training in the 'big picture' horizons offered by philosophy and history. In one sense, this is just a Platonic gloss on the slogan, 'Correlation is not causation'. However, in practice, it helps to explain the dedication of Fabians and Progressives to social science methodologies based on designing living laboratories, the basis for so-called 'policy-relevant research'. This is the only form of empirical research that they – and their neo-liberal descendants – have ever taken seriously. Two figures from the Great Society era of the 1960s who would fall into this category were the social psychologist Donald Campbell and the sociologist James Coleman, both of whom thought of theorizing as the process of designing 'smart environments' to enable people to reach optimal solutions given their hypothesized capacities and liabilities. The latest version of this line of thought to appeal to policymakers on both sides of the Atlantic has been 'nudge' (Thaler and Sunstein 2008).

3 SEEING THE UNIVERSITY THROUGH NEO-LIBERAL EYES

In the UK context, we are witnessing a long hangover from the heady days of inflated expectations – starting with the Robbins Report – of what a proliferation of universities might achieve in terms of growing 21st-century Britain. However, the economic logic behind it was impeccable: a fair exchange for the state raising university student numbers and research provision to unprecedented levels is that the public purse is provided with an adequate regular return on these investments. Even tuition fees should be understood in this 'pump priming' way. While Old Leftists (some of them young in years) still fixate on the conversion of a 'basic human right' (aka free education) to an 'exchange relation' (aka tuition fees), they would do better to appreciate the amount of faith (and capital) in the promise of a 'knowledge-based economy' that the neo-liberal state has invested in university-based activities. The bare fact that university fees were raised to £9,000 per annum – understood as state-backed loans – is less important than the belief that students would ever earn enough to pay them back (McGettigan 2013).

Nevertheless, it is true that if you are a neo-liberal administrator (as opposed to an Academic Caesar), academics are no more – but no less – than major players in a more generic knowledge market. What exactly this means has been examined in Mirowski (2002), which considers the post-Second World War spread of the Shannon-Weaver entropy-based model of communication, which defines 'information' as whatever it is about a message that reduces uncertainty in the receiver such that he or she is thereby enabled to take a decision. To unpack Gregory Bateson's famous slogan: It is the difference (from what might otherwise be expected from the sender) that makes a difference (to the decision taken by the receiver). Economically speaking, this effectively equates knowledge content with use value, hence making academia ripe for market analysis of the sort that produces metrics for the 'value-added' of degrees and the 'user group impact' of research. It follows that the relative success or failure of academia in its pump-priming functions could be turned over to public relations firms capable of gauging levels of uptake, associated attitudes, as well as long-term impact in the target markets. Of course, the state would need to possess a clear sense of what would count as 'success', the standards of which would be developed in consultation with academics but ultimately administered independently of them by these firms.

There was much consternation in UK academia in the summer of 2015 about the Department for Business, Innovation and Skills' commissioning of McKinsey consultants to audit its operating budget (Wilsdon 2015). McKinsey is the champion of the 'leaner and meaner' corporate profile. This means starting the audit by looking at strategic goals, not ongoing operations. One does not presume that the latter necessarily advance the former. In particular, in some vague pursuit of 'fairness' (= minimizing employee blowback), firms are always tempted to make similar 'across the board' cuts, even if in the long term this further impedes their meeting strategic goals. However, as McKinsey regularly observes, making quite deep but targeted cuts may enable new productive synergies. Academia may be well suited to this sort of treatment.

Anyone who thinks seriously about state funding for academic research realizes the centrality of 'basic research' to generate the capital that underwrites the next generation of innovations. On this basis alone, research is clearly a 'public good'. Moreover, in recent years, major science policy players have been quite imaginative in their interpretation of this point, most notably the 'converging technologies' agenda launched by the US National Science Foundation in 2002 and imitated worldwide (Roco and Bainbridge 2002). This proposal would have the state provide incentives for emerging developments in the nano-, bio-, info- and cogno- sciences and technologies to be mutually oriented with an overarching long-term aim of 'enhancing human performance', understood quite broadly from classic social democratic goals of improving worker health and productivity to more transhumanist goals of extending human life expectancy indefinitely (Fuller 2011: chap. 3). What the President of Arizona State University, Michael Crow, calls 'The New American University' has been from the start attuned to this policy initiative (Crow and Dabars 2015: chap. 7).

However, even in matters of basic research, it does not follow that discipline-based committees of 'peers' are the best way to decide the direction of policy travel. The broadest level of assent to the value of peer review is as a mechanism for catching and correcting errors of various sorts. Any larger claims to peer review's value is subject to significant controversy, which is largely masked by the fact that peer review (starting at the journal level) is also the main vehicle through which disciplinary identity is reproduced. However, from the state's standpoint, it is an open question whether reproducing existing disciplinary structures is the best way to promote basic research – especially given that basic research generally thrives in an interdisciplinary environment, where researchers are not burdened by the often idiosyncratic ('path-dependent') epistemic trajectories which have been taken by particular fields. Thus, we may need 'smart metrics' capable of surveying the entire research environment to demonstrate how researchers are voting with their feet, in terms of who, how and why they cite of their fellows. ('Altmetrics' is one cyber-friendly version.) On this basis, projections can then be made about the likely consequences of various resource allocation schemes. The state can then finally think about research investment in a more 'business-like' manner – and not simply as an extended version of the 'old boys club'.

To be sure, peer review can look like the path of least resistance for all concerned in matters of knowledge policy. At least since the time of Margaret Thatcher, UK academics have been relatively easily co-opted into all manner of higher education innovations, not least the exercise now called the 'Research Excellence Framework' – just as long as they were the ones administering them. Academic opposition to such paradigmatically neo-liberal innovations follows a predictable arc: an initial loud period quickly reveals the absence of a coherent positive alternative that commands the support of the majority of the noise-makers. Practical opposition then disappears, with some academics returning to business as usual, while others – self-described as being on the political 'left' – make careers by adding 'depth' to the predicament, which amounts to rationalizations for why opposing the direction of policy travel will always fail, pending some miraculous strafing of the policy fields.

Nevertheless, seen in the harsh light that neo-liberalism shines, academics are simply being indulged in their worst tendencies by being allowed to administer such state-sponsored experiments. Here, I recall something that David Willetts used to say when UK Minister for Universities in the Conservative-Liberal coalition government of 2010–15, which always struck me as generous but somewhat misguided. He said that the reason the government relied on peer review rather than metrics to assess academic research – despite the additional costs and inconvenience – was that the academics themselves insisted on it. While this is very much in line with academic compliance behaviour, it is not obvious that the government's strategic goals were being well served in what is admitted by all sides to be such a wasteful process as peer review. To be sure, given the existing hostility that most academics express towards metrics of any sort, incentives will be needed to engage the full range of academic intelligence required for the evaluative task to be performed adequately (i.e. not just those who enjoy crunching numbers).

The endgame of this process is that disciplines would no longer be the basis on which research monies are allocated – and so, for example, one should expect a greater cross-disciplinary consolidation of the research funding councils. To be sure, disciplines would continue to play a significant role as market signals for students wishing to enter university (as well as the basis of their training), and peer review will continue to function in journals as the premier error-eliminating mechanism in the organized knowledge system. None of this would prevent particular universities or academic societies from promoting certain disciplines as free-standing epistemic entities. However, the state's role in their promotion is not obvious.

On the teaching side, in that UK context, the neo-liberal state would ideally work towards an arrangement whereby all universities are given complete corporate autonomy (aka privatized) – with the exception of Oxford and Cambridge, which should remain 'nationalized', at least for the foreseeable future. They are proven global brand leaders for the UK that would not be able to compete at their current levels (i.e. *vis-à-vis* the US Ivy League) without government subsidy. However, as long as Oxbridge enjoys this privileged fiscal status, it needs to be monitored for its proactivity in locating high talent, especially in the most unsuspecting school districts. As for the rest of the universities, it may come to pass that in this 'freer' environment, some may merge or disappear altogether if they fail to find a market. In the context, the government should dedicate significant funds to universities that demonstrate 'value-added' to their students, typically meaning levels of achievement that exceed intake expectations.

How exactly this 'added value' is measured is bound to be contentious but necessary, in terms of the state's overall strategy of treating higher education as a vehicle for human capital development. One beneficial effect may be that university rankings are steered away from measures that reflect purely input (e.g. admissions scores) or purely output (e.g. job placements) to ones that reflect input-output ratios. Indeed, the question that both Academic Caesars and neo-liberal administrators should ask is: Which universities have added the most value to the students attending them? Which have done the most with the least by enabling its students to beat the odds in life's lottery? Michael Crow, whose Arizona State University is located in one of America's fastest-growing and most diverse regions, has placed this question at the heart of the 'New American University' (Crow and Dabars 2015: chap. 1). I return to this question of the 'added value' of a university education in the final chapter of this book with a discussion of what I call the *proactionary university*.

4 THE NEO-LIBERAL CHALLENGE TO THE ACADEMIC CAESAR: HOW TO DEMONSTRATE THE VALUE ADDED OF UNIVERSITIES TO SOCIETY

The bottom line question that the state asks of universities is their 'value added' to the society which funds them. In light of recent budgetary constraints, the question has been put rather pointedly: Would society suffer from lower levels of public expenditure – and what would make greater public expenditure worthwhile? To be sure, these are quite reasonable questions to ask, given that even today most of the people whose taxes go to funding universities have never set foot on a campus.

A university-based education promises more than to enable students to pass exams and acquire credentials. It exposes them to cutting-edge research in their chosen field of study – even if that calls into question some of the exam answers that they might be asked. Moreover, university-based researchers in the proper 'Humboldtian' mould take their work to be of value not merely to like-minded researchers but, at least in principle, to any interested intelligent person, including those sceptical of the fundamental premises of that research. Indeed, the test of a true academic lies in the capacity to deconstruct one's own epistemic authority. Just to be clear: this capacity has nothing to do with the sort of self-reflexive critique that is often mistaken for radical thinking in postmodernist circles. In fact, it is almost the exact opposite. *Self-vulgarization* captures what I mean: one's knowledge claims can be explained so that someone without the same credentials can understand, contest and possibly extend them. In this way, the classroom becomes a crucible for democracy, as people from diverse backgrounds come to understand that the power that comes from knowledge is not the exclusive preserve of those who had the privilege or luck to have followed a certain intellectual trajectory.

At this point let us return to Ernst & Young's move to circumvent academia altogether in its recruitment process by administering purpose-made examinations. This is an attempt to produce a more targeted and less expensive version of what it – and much of society – thinks is the source of value in a university education. To be sure, exams have always sat uneasily between the teaching and research functions of the university. At best, exams capture a student's ability to provide a snapshot of a field in motion. But photography is a medium better suited for the dead or the immortal than for ongoing inquiry, where a premium is placed on the prospect that many of our future beliefs will be substantially different from our present ones.

A recurring theme in the life stories of great innovators of the modern period, notably Einstein, is the failure of the exam system to bring out their true capacities. It is not that the thinking of these innovators had not been transformed by their academic experience. Rather, it is that academia lacked an adequate means of registering that transformation. One charitable but not implausible diagnosis of many of the errors routinely picked up by academic examiners is that they result from students having suspended conventional assumptions in the field in which they are being examined. Yet, these assumptions may themselves be challenged if not overturned in the not-too-distant future. Thus, what strikes the examiner as corner-cutting sloppiness may capture an intuition that is the basis for a more efficient grasp of the truth of some matter.

But what sort of examination system would vindicate this charitable reading of error and thereby aid in spotting the next generation of innovators? It is not obvious that an in-house exam administered by, say, Ernst & Young will be any less of an epistemic snapshot than an academic exam, if it simply tests for the ability to solve normal puzzles in normal ways. The in-house exam will simply be more content-relevant to the employer. An alternative would be to make all university examinations tests in counterfactual reasoning. In effect, students would be provided access to the field's current state of knowledge – the sort of thing that they would normally regurgitate as exam answers – and then be asked to respond to scenarios in which the assumptions behind the answers are suspended in various ways. Thus, students would be tested at once for their sense of how the current state of knowledge hangs together and their ability to reassemble that knowledge strategically under a state of induced uncertainty. This would be to examine in the spirit of Humboldt.

Does the ability to do well on such exams add sufficient value to society to make the university worthy of sustained and dedicated public (or, for that matter, private) funding? Needless to say, flesh-and-blood academics all too often fall short in setting a proper example in either their pedagogical or research practice. But the state's balance sheet also bears a major share of the blame. As long as universities derive a significant part of their income from addressing teaching and research as separate matters, administrators will try to game the system to maximize each function separately in their hiring decisions and internal allocation of resources. Indeed, this tendency may be the biggest long-term threat to the university's corporate integrity.

But why should the state, as the custodian of society, be interested in sustaining the teacher-researcher role that underwrites the university's corporate integrity? Consider the talk about the need to foster a 'climate of innovation'. Fidelity to the concept requires more than using the word 'innovation' a lot and boosting each and every crazy idea to paradigm-shifting status. Rather, it involves the public's exposure – both in and out of the classroom – to people who embody the dynamic rush of intellectual life yet manage to bring it into focus so as to live up to the Enlightenment motto, 'Knowledge is power'. These people – 'academics' in Humboldt's original sense – inspire by pointing the way forward (cf. Collins 1998: chap. 12). They routinely move others away from their comfort zones, as they move themselves from their own. It is in this deep sense that universities provide a 'climate of innovation' which merits continued state support. But who is capable of leading such people? Enter the Academic Caesar.

I

UNIVERSITY LEADERSHIP IN THE 21ST CENTURY: THE CASE FOR ACADEMIC CAESARISM

1 SOME STAGE-SETTING FOR THE ACADEMIC CAESAR

The Academic Caesar is no faceless Hobbesian Leviathan but the face of the general will as per democratic dictators of the sort that Rousseau could love. But perhaps even more than a dictator, the Academic Caesar's personality must draw from the university's past to project the institution into a future that challenges its current members to respond productively. Generally speaking, the US has fostered Academic Caesarism much more effectively than anywhere else, combining an often prophetic style of leadership, based on the independent church origins of the first American colleges, and a Humboldtian orientation to the university as a builder of both individual character and national identity.

Universities have historically exerted power by holding a state-licensed monopoly in knowledge legitimation. This has been manifested in various ways over the centuries: the training of administrative elites, the certification of school curricula, as well as housing the principal means by which advanced knowledge is authorized, documented and disseminated. A scarcity of universities has historically abetted this multiplex sense of monopoly. Yet universities have also always relied on extramural sources for income, be it current and past students or private and public agencies. Such a diverse funding environment has led to conflicting demands for corporate accountability. This state of affairs has been exacerbated over the past half-century by the creation of many more universities, expected to do more things while being allowed to draw from a wider range of potential funders. Indeed, this state of affairs had been already foreseen – and largely embraced – by, say, Kerr (1963). The logic of this development points towards universities expanding their scope of governance in society as they increase the scale of their operations, in a manner not so different from the evolution of business firms into transnational corporations in the 20th century. The Academic Caesar needs to decide whether this model is sustainable for his or her own institution – though clearly it has been for, say, Harvard (Bok 1982: esp. chap. 8).

In the standard narratives of neo-liberal knowledge production, the university straddles two fates. At best the university is portrayed as a supple organism adaptive to a fluid environment. At worst it appears as a living fossil artificially maintained by a declining national support system. However, there is an alternative way to think about the university's current predicament, one that draws more deeply from the university's common legal ancestry with the state, the church and – latterly – the firm. It involves the embodiment of the institution's corporate personality in the style of academic leadership I call 'Academic Caesarism', a phrase designed to draw attention to both the promise and the peril of universities' acquiring leaders who so strongly identify with their institution that they may feel they must protect its identity even from its own academic constituency.

The university is related to the state in an historically twofold fashion. On the one hand, both the university and the state (more exactly, the city-state) acquired their organizational autonomy under medieval Roman law in much the same way – that is, as instances of *universitas*, normally translated as 'corporation'. Indeed, the ordinary use of 'corporation' to refer to universities and states (and guilds and churches) predates its use for business firms by at least five centuries. On the other hand, most actual universities in the modern era (outside the US) were founded as institutions of the state, designed to consolidate national identity by providing a crucible for forging the next generation of society's leaders. In either case, the legal status of *universitas* implied that these corporate entities were 'artificial persons', whose autonomy consists in pursuing their own ends, as distinct from those of the particular individuals who constitute this artificial person at any given point. Aside from a sense of self-direction, the university's corporate autonomy is also defined in terms of the self-selection of its members and the self-organization of its activities, including the provision of material support.

Not surprisingly, given this history, the legitimacy of both the state and the university has come under attack in these postmodern, neo-liberal times. The attacks are most directly felt in terms of the provision of material support, where both have been subject to a shrinkage in discretionary public sector funding. At a more conceptual level, the attacks on the legitimacy of the university and the state have also pursued a parallel course: postmodern attacks on the university's ability to represent and integrate knowledge resemble neo-liberal attacks on the state's ability to represent and integrate people (Lyotard 1983). At the same time, many universities have adjusted to postmodernism and neo-liberalism by acquiring functions previously reserved to the state. A precedent for this tendency can be found in US universities, many of which – including most of the Ivy League – had been established as autonomous institutions prior to American national independence. While it is easy to dismiss the US experience as exceptional, in fact it serves as a reminder of the medieval origins of universities and states as legal siblings. In this respect, the US may provide clues on how universities may reassert their autonomy as state-like institutions.

The practical implications of universities acquiring state-like functions are epitomized in two phrases: *Academic Imperialism* and *Academic Caesarism.* The former refers to the tendency for universities to absorb the state's welfare functions, e.g. the provision and regulation of healthcare, education and perhaps even domestic security. The latter refers to a leadership style among university chief executives that resembles a dictator who extends his or her institutional authority while both protecting and limiting the power exerted by a group of potentially divisive constituencies. In what follows, I shall develop the concept of Academic Imperialism through that of Academic Caesarism, following the historic pattern of ancient Rome.

Like Athens in its classical period, republican Rome treated citizenship as the measure of equality in society. In particular, all citizens were equally invested in the republic's well-being, by virtue of having owned and managed property there for several generations. This created a presumption of roughly equal willingness and ability to take dictatorial powers, whenever there was a need for the republic to take action against a common enemy. Such states of emergency were assumed to be temporary, after which the dictator would resume his ordinary life as a citizen. However, as Rome expanded its borders, eventually to overseas colonies, the dictator's role metamorphosed from an office that, at least in principle, any citizen could hold to an office worthy only of people possessing special qualities required for the role's expanded scope. Thus, as the republic became an empire, the dictator became a Caesar (Baehr 2008: chap. 2).

A similar trajectory can be charted in the history of the university, whose republican phase corresponds to institutional governance on a collegial basis. Here the leader would be expected to have come up the academic ranks in the same or comparable institution. Indeed, Oxbridge and the US Ivy League often seem to operate with a default policy of hiring their own graduates. It is easy nowadays to dismiss this practice as simply so much academic snobbery, if not outright nepotism. However, the practice harks back to the university's legal status as an artificial person, where intellectual lineage acquires the role of biological lineage in natural persons. Thus, each new university matriculant is portrayed as born anew – hence, the university's personification as *alma mater*, 'nurturing mother'. In this respect, the university's entrance examinations and degree certifications are comparable to baptism and holy orders, respectively, as initiation rites in the church, another of the university's institutional siblings. Both sets of rites require that individuals undergo a trial of faith, the successful outcome of which is the acquisition of a new identity as part of the larger corporate structure.

Just as Rome's self-understanding underwent a gradual transformation from republic to empire – bracketed by the careers of Julius and Augustus Caesar – so too has the university's. The university's imperial phase began when the institution diversified its functions to such an extent that satisfying the interests of its official 'citizenry' (i.e. academics on the payroll and perhaps enrolled students) constituted only part of the task of maintaining the institution's autonomy. I allude here to the university's proto-state activities, ranging from economic pump-priming through the provision of welfare, both typically at the local regional level, to more client-centred delivery of skills, products and services. In this context, the university's stakeholders expand to approximate the range that would normally have an interest in the decisions taken by a state assembly.

Some universities – including the US land-grant colleges and the universities created in the Global South under European imperial rule – were specifically chartered in anticipation of their expanded capacity. They are not unreasonably seen as governing in lieu of the state, in terms that both universities and states have found more-or-less mutually satisfying. Where the states saw the universities as organizing regions and recruiting leaders, the universities saw the states as licensing the extension of their research activities in the name of 'development'. (Indeed, the term 'extension' is still used in the US in this context.) Not surprisingly, with the decline of both state power in the first world and imperial power in the third world, universities created in this imperial mode have acquired still more state-like functions, sometimes even serving as *de facto* alternative governments.

Nevertheless, some universities, including Oxbridge and the US Ivy League, have drawn out the transition from republic to empire in their self-understanding – though not their actual functions – as long as possible. They have perpetuated the image that the university's chief executive is really a *primus inter pares*, even though his or her decisions extend to matters way beyond what those who normally roam the campus might see as being in their own best interests. Not surprisingly, serious cracks increasingly appear in the image, as became clear in the first decade of the current century, when both Oxford and Harvard made controversial chief executive appointments, both of which ended in tears within five years.

First, consider John Hood, Oxford's first vice chancellor to have been chosen from outside its own academic faculties in the university's 900-year history. A Rhodes Scholar from New Zealand, whose only Oxford degree is an M.Phil. in Management, Hood's appointment received the enthusiastic support of Oxford's chancellor Chris Patten, a Tory modernizer who wanted to reorganize the university's medieval corporate structure, specifically by separating and streamlining the academic and financial functions – in both cases, shifting power from the colleges to the departments and central administration, as per most modern universities. Hood had achieved something comparable at the University of Auckland, which he catapulted into the top 100 of world universities as vice chancellor.

However, things did not work out so smoothly at Oxford. The speed with which he attempted to transform its time-honoured traditions gave the impression of disrespect and self-aggrandizement. Yet, despite suffering major setbacks from the 'Congregation', as Oxford's senate is called, Hood's efforts at reform enjoyed the support of roughly 40% of the academic staff and most of the students and alumni, who constitute the greater Oxford community. However, in the end, Hood's position was untenable and, tellingly, the term of his successor, an American chemist, was conspicuous by the absence of any discernible academic leadership.

An equally clear case of the difficulties facing universities as they shift from republican to imperial mode is captured in the saga of Larry Summers, whose tenure as Harvard president came to an ignominious end in 2006. Unlike Hood, whose last appearance at Oxford prior to his appointment was as a first-class cricketer for the university team thirty years earlier, Summers had been one of the youngest tenured professors at Harvard, a recipient of the main professional award for economists under the age of forty. A lifelong Democrat, Summers was appointed chief economist at the World Bank and then Secretary of the Treasury in rapid succession when Bill Clinton was US President. However, Summers returned to Harvard after the election of Republican George W. Bush, now as the university's president. By all accounts, Summers' management style was to dictate without consultation, presuming that as himself a 'Harvard man' there was no need to solicit opinion more widely. On his own, then, Summers continued Harvard's famed international outreach and development programmes, while stressing the university's traditional emphasis on a broad undergraduate liberal education to which its distinguished faculty were expected to contribute regularly and responsibly.

These policies made Summers very popular with students and alumni, who increased their financial support to this richest of universities. But they also earned him the enmity of tenured academics. In more high-minded mode, they objected to Harvard's global meddling, which in the 1990s, under Jeffrey Sachs' directorship of the Institute for International Development, had promoted a radical liberalization of former Soviet-style economies. But equally as important as a source of opposition, Summers challenged the informal policy of tenured academics offloading their teaching to untenured colleagues and graduate students. However, the tipping point against Summers came when he openly admitted that evolutionary psychologists might be correct about a possible genetic basis for women's inferior scientific performance. Although colleagues such as Steven Pinker came to Summers' defence, this politically incorrect utterance provided a rhetorical pretext for the faculty to declare that they could not work under someone with such odious views. As it turns out, Summers' permanent successor, Drew Gilpin Faust, is not only the first woman but also, and more remarkably in the American context, the first non-Harvard-trained person to become its president since the university's founding in 1636 – albeit she was already running the university's Institute for Advanced Studies.

These two vignettes of less-than-best practice, combined with the more general historical and theoretical considerations about Caesarism as a mode of governance, suggest the following five defining features of a successful Academic Caesar (AC):

1 The AC is a university president (or rector, vice chancellor) who regards his or her role as comparable to a chief executive officer of a major corporation, i.e. an agent ultimately responsible to a diverse set of principals ('stakeholders'), including academics, students, alumni, the general public and, where relevant, a board of trustees and/or state legislature. But even if the AC is not currently a practising academic, s/he should be sufficiently connected to academic culture to be able to easily articulate the university's goals in ways that practising academics can recognize as reflective of their own values and aspirations.

2 Nevertheless, the AC believes that only someone in his or her position is competent to take decisions concerning overall university policy. The AC is not a *primus inter pares* but in a class by him- or herself. On the one hand, the AC enjoys an epistemic advantage over more discipline-based academics in a scaled-up competitive environment that forces one to

deal with many more non-academics, as well as academics who are not primarily moved by disciplinary imperatives. On the other hand, despite the traditional standing of academic self-governance, divisiveness, if not outright fecklessness, better characterizes academic conduct in matters of university governance, which in turn produces the vacuum of leadership that the AC gladly fills.

3. When the AC's actions elicit opposition from the university's constituencies, s/he can deftly distinguish the values and ideals upheld by his/her institution from the various interests of those constituencies, including current academic staff. The AC has a very clear sense of the difference between institutional autonomy and individual (or group) selfishness – and can turn that difference to his/her advantage. Thus, the AC may be inclined to take a strong stand against the establishment of academic fiefdoms while strongly defending the academic freedom of an unpopular colleague. Since even universally endorsed academic values can be – and have been – taken in multiple contradictory or incommensurable directions, the AC can gain and maintain power simply by upholding this plurality, thereby preventing any particular interpretation of those values from becoming dominant. Thus, the AC's hand is naturally strengthened *vis-à-vis* particular constituencies by expanding their number, not least through 'affirmative action'.

4. The AC is happy to allow the university's various constituencies to pursue their interests freely, on the condition that they do not interfere with the AC's efforts to maintain the material conditions of their freedom. Thus, the AC is not above 'channelling' the interests of principals in ways that decrease the likelihood that they will interfere with the AC's tasks. For example, when alumni demand a greater say in university governance, they are offered surveys whose influence on university policy is indeterminate, or sports teams whose matches serve as a safety valve for expressing their commitment to *alma mater*. It amounts to a strategy of 'bread and circuses'.

5. Nevertheless, the AC must also maintain a clear distinction between the university's 'internal' and 'external' constituencies – say, on the one hand, academic staff, students and alumni, and on the other, representatives of politics, business, etc. This is how a university in the imperial mode retains its republican core, and the AC can legitimize his/her exercise of power in terms of the protection of institutional autonomy. Thus, the AC must prevent external constituencies from unduly influencing the governance of the internal constituencies, say, by allowing a large client-oriented grant to

an academic department to set a standard to which other departments are then held accountable. Rather, the AC should see such grants as, in the first instance, upsetting the institution's equilibrium, which of course need not be negative. However, the AC must then use grant overheads creatively to engage in compensation or redistribution across the institution.

In the rest of the chapter, I explore this last feature of Academic Caesarism by elaborating its underlying political economy, which envisages the university as part church and part casino, possessing what I later call 'a Vatican face and a Vegas Heart'. In short, the successful Academic Caesar upholds his/her institution's autonomy by securing and expanding the material base that can sustain the most intellectual adventure within its borders possible. On the one hand, this feat requires an imaginative forward-looking macro-economic strategy, which is detailed in the next three sections, including a discussion and critique of the internal opposition, which I regard as a form of rentier capitalism. On the other hand, it also calls on the Academic Caesar to make the university less directly sensitive to market pressures by reasserting its epistemic distinctiveness as offering a second-order, or public, good, in terms of which other forms of private and first-order knowledge may be evaluated and regulated. This topic, the Academic Caesar's 'ultimate weapon', is discussed in the final section.

2 THE NEO-LIBERAL ENVIRONMENT AS A BREEDING GROUND FOR ACADEMIC CAESARS

When he was still a working sociologist and not director of the London School of Economics, Craig Calhoun (2006) challenged higher education thinkers, practitioners and researchers to come up with a business plan for today's university that demonstrates that only by adhering to classical academic norms it can effectively serve the social and economic ends increasingly demanded of the institution. My proposal, addressed to the aspiring Academic Caesar, starts from the perhaps counterintuitive assumption that whatever model of political economy is used to rationalize the university these days, it tends *not* to be based on 'productivity', that is, the efficient translation of labour and capital into goods and services. To be sure, the rhetoric surrounding the 'entrepreneurial university', not to mention the pervasive and casual use of the phrase 'knowledge production', appears indebted to this model (Clark 1998, Gibbons et al. 1994). Nevertheless, the resemblance is superficial – a conflation of (doubtless) *increased production* and (doubtful) *increased productivity*.

While our speech may be confused, our actions are loud and clear: the main academic performance indicators are based not on productivity but sheer production – of students (enrolled, graduated, or employed), research (funded, published, patented, or cited), income (received or generated), etc. The dominance of cumulative over ratio metrics in the various 'league tables' (a UK football-based expression corresponding to 'rankings' in the US) of universities proves the point. By these standards, the United States is the world's sole academic superpower and its undisputed capital is Harvard.

But is the US the most *productive* academic nation-state? This is a sensitive matter in the United Kingdom, where higher education has been repeatedly congratulated for doing more with fewer resources: a model of neo-liberal productivity (e.g. May 1997). For the last quarter-century, the UK has been arguably the most productive academic nation on Earth. For example, the combined endowment and annual income of Harvard is seven times that of Oxford and Cambridge combined. Is Harvard *seven* times better than Oxbridge? Maybe two or three times, but surely not seven! Perhaps unsurprisingly, as an American who has now lived in the UK for more than twenty years, my kneejerk response upon returning to a US campus is to observe the plush resources that go wasted or underutilized by tenured academics who quaintly fuss over the content of their courses as preludes to research they might conduct someday. The US is the world's largest academic producer by virtue of being its most conspicuous consumer.

I call my response 'kneejerk' so as not to belittle the American norm, which, despite many local challenges, remains reasonably robust. On the contrary, the success of US-style conspicuous consumption in academia reveals an important, albeit complex, truth: that universities are institutions that produce with impunity. Classical ways of thinking about this phenomenon usually include the image of following the trail of truth wherever it may lead. This image is taken from the bygone era of what Derek de Solla Price (1963) called 'little science', where the main resources were one's own time, energy, and money – not great amounts of equipment, manpower, and other people's money. The image is continuous with the political economy implicit in Aristotle's injunction to turn to 'philosophy' (a proxy for any systematic intellectual inquiry) only once the household chores were done. To recall a point Marxists used to relish, Aristotle treated philosophy as quite literally a kind of mental gymnastics that was not expected, any more than competitive sports, to feed back into the relief of humanity's secular burdens. Rather, it was the consummate leisured activity, one devoted to contemplating how and why the world is as it is.

This attitude has persisted in the West well into the modern era, even as it came into conflict with Muslim, Christian, and ultimately Enlightenment ideologies of knowledge as a collective legacy and universal entitlement for the betterment of humanity, indeed, perhaps to create 'a heaven on earth'. In *The Decline and Fall of the Roman Empire*, Edward Gibbon (2000) may have demonized Caliph Omar as philistine for casting all of ancient wisdom to the flames when he torched the Library of Alexandria in 640 AD, yet similar feelings of contempt were expressed by his own contemporaries – including such Enlightenment icons as Hume and Smith, Voltaire and Diderot – towards the 'useless' knowledge then amassed in European universities. The existence of tomes produced in the name of 'curiosity' written in languages few could understand and to which even fewer would have access manifested the intellectual equivalent of greed, a mortal sin for the faithful and idle capital for everyone else. Embarrassingly, good economic sense informs this philistine contempt, which can often be found among neo-liberal administrators today. However, the concept of 'undiscovered public knowledge', introduced in the next chapter, offers a more constructive approach to the problem which the Caliph solved by igniting a bonfire of the vanities.

Nevertheless, the most efficient means for a state to improve its citizenry's stock of human capital for purposes of increasing overall national wealth is to invest in primary and secondary education, even at the expense of higher education and original research (Wolf 2002). And if the state must invest in university teaching and research at all, the national interest is best served by an investment strategy that encourages free access between academics and those capable of turning their ideas into transferable skills and marketable products. After all, no number of showcase research institutes can compensate for mass deficiencies in basic literacy and numeracy, and no number of registered patents can replace direct involvement in industrial research and development. It is often forgotten that Humboldt himself had such a joined-up strategy to the different education sectors and how they might inform national development. It follows that a budget-conscious state keen on making its mark in the world's increasingly knowledge-based economy would adopt a two-pronged strategy towards higher education.

First, the state would redistribute education funding from the tertiary to the primary and secondary levels, so that people can acquire the requisite competitive skills as early as possible, thereby assuring quick and decisive entry into a globalized labour market. This strategy would help to counteract 'credentials creep', the need for each new generation of students to spend more time in formal schooling to acquire comparable qualifications. While it follows that fewer people would initially require university training (or if so, for a shorter period), the innovation-induced volatility of the global knowledge economy ensures that whatever financial losses universities incur in the short term will be recovered later through recidivism (aka 'lifelong learning') whereby late-breaking skills are acquired by those not lucky enough to have been originally exposed to them. In this respect, ambient incentives to generate innovation are like temptations to commit crime or susceptibilities to suffer illness: that is, persuasive justifications for the public funding of what Erving Goffman (1961) called 'total institutions'. Universities can thus position themselves in the market next to prisons and hospitals as 'social equilibrium providers'.

The second prong of the state's strategy would be to maintain the porosity of the boundary dividing academia from industry and the private sector more generally. This would probably lead to a widening of the variance in academic salaries, perhaps decoupling them from academic rank altogether. Universities could adopt the British practice of justifying further public expenditure by pointing out the diminishing burden they place on taxpayers to fund their activities, as academics accumulate grants, patents, consultancies, and so forth. In the long term, universities might even renounce their non-profit legal status, assuming they could persuade their trustees and perhaps alumni to think of themselves as corporate shareholders – and academics to think of themselves as employees.

Even in these neo-liberal times, universities can be more than suppliers of capital – both human (in education) and non-human (in research) – for the global knowledge economy. But that does not mean that they should stand above – or outside – economic considerations. Rather, universities should lead rather than follow, which is the *raison d'être* of the Academic Caesar. Combining Humboldt and Joseph Schumpeter, the grand theorist of entrepreneurship, I have elsewhere defined the unique corporate function of the university as the 'creative destruction of social capital' (Fuller 2003). By this phrase I mean to update the dynamic unity that Humboldt held to exist between education and research, which I would now characterize as alternating phases of an endless cycle. Humboldt's innovation was to turn the university into an engine of social progress – specifically, progress of the 'nation', the spirit of which state policy tries to embody, however imperfectly. Schumpeter, writing over a century later, recognized that the universities have been the most reliable, and sometimes effective, source of anti-establishment thought (Schumpeter 1942: chap. 13).

Research initially generates social capital by forging new alliances between ideas, people, processes, and things. However, a university dedicated purely, or even primarily, to research would simply polarize the populace between, so to speak, the 'knows' and the 'know-nots', a kind of epistemological feudalism. But luckily, here the teaching function enters to level this emergent difference by spreading the fruits of research as widely as possible. Significantly, students are often far from the original networks responsible for the research in which they are being instructed, but their appreciation is vital for its continued social support and, more importantly, for taking the research in unexpected directions. This, in turn, will forge new alliances and redistribute competitive advantage across society.

In effect, the soul of the university as the creative destroyer of social capital resides in curriculum committees empowered with deciding which aspects of new research are worth incorporating into, say, a discipline-based major or a general liberal arts requirement. In this respect, the 'canon wars' that have been fought in the humanities faculties of US campuses for at least thirty years merely bring a level of self-consciousness and media attention to a process that has been endemic to the modern history of the university. The only difference now is that possibly the amount and rate of replacement of course content is greater than in the past. If true, this might be a reflection of the enlarged and diversified student body of recent years, the composition of which can more easily conjure up the idea that society's future should be significantly different from its past.

There is a model for this ever-expanding and forward-looking vision of the university. It is the oldest legally incorporated private sector entity, the self-supporting *church*, out of which the original universities evolved in the 12th century. The economic side of proselytism is that church finances typically flow 'forward' not 'backward'. Rather than requiring potential converts to pay upfront to join a church before they have received any benefits (however defined), those whose lives have been already transformed by their membership in a community of faith donate some percentage of their subsequent income to allow others to share in the same fellowship. Thus, instead of preaching the academic faith themselves, the donors trust their alma maters to do it for them. This attitude towards universities is uniquely anchored in the United States because of the nation's origins in British religious dissenters. Consequently, by any world standard, even officially state-funded universities enjoy enviable alumni contributions that enable them to retain a large measure of their institutional autonomy, even in the face of external economic and political pressures.

Two features of this autonomy are worth highlighting: the university's discretion to select a considerable number of students who cannot pay anything near full tuition costs, and to permit a considerable number of faculty members to survive on relatively low research productivity. Ideally, such students will turn out to be generous alumni, and such faculty inspiring teachers. Of course, neither ideal is always realized. Nevertheless, generous alumni tend to invoke inspiring teachers – not the acquisition of job-related skills – as motivating their endowments. Moreover, these alumni will typically not have been the most promising students, nor the teachers they invoke especially productive researchers. This suggests that at least some, if not most, American universities have designed a successful long-term financial strategy based on the 'spirit' rather than 'matter' of their institutions. Thus, the values upheld by the student donors turn out to converge with those of the regular faculty. Put in blunt business terms: customer and employee satisfaction are at joint equilibrium.

This argument raises a more general point of relevance to the Academic Caesar's strategic vision. Although academics constitute only one of several constituencies vying for the Academic Caesar's favour, they are the ones best poised to help or harm the university's corporate brand. And while research plays an important role in this process, as more research takes place off campus and even outside the scrutiny of academia's peer-review process, teaching becomes increasingly important to distinguish the university from other knowledge-producing agents. In the Introduction to this book, I broached the issue in relation to how examinations demonstrate (or not) the 'value added' of academic instruction. But turning to the core teaching activity, the lecture, we find that savvier elite institutions have already begun to transfer their dominance by providing online courses that are licensed for broadcast to non-elite universities. This development goes under the general name of 'MOOC': that is, 'massive open online course'. Although many MOOCs simply consist of a curated selection of purpose-made and off-the-shelf video clips, the mass distribution of Michael Sandel's (2010) Harvard undergraduate course on the nature of justice began to focus minds on the potential challenge that MOOCs provide to traditional modes of content delivery in higher education (Kolowich 2013).

Whatever else one might say about the MOOC, which is very much a work in progress, it raises the question of why non-elite universities need elaborate grounds to maintain their activities, when lectures by top academics in their fields can be seen (at a price) on one's laptop, followed by digitally communicated assignments and assessments, as enhanced by periodic contact with 'learning support personnel' specially trained to get students through the epistemic speed bumps. Add to the mix the increasing casualization of academic labour, and the Academic Caesar may be tempted to downsize the university's physical plant, say, by explicitly selling residence halls, offices and classroom space, or – less obtrusively – render everything 'dual purpose' so that they can be 'time-shared' between academic and non-academic activities. But it is not clear that the university can survive merely as a concept without a strong sense of place, symbolized by the commons or 'campus' that is an attractor for students. But this may involve the Academic Caesar in the toughest battle of all – namely, to persuade academics themselves that they should be a living presence on campus, especially in the classroom, which remains the best place to sell the university as an institution worthy of sustained support.

To think about this problem, consider the shift from the theatre to the home as the site for experiencing the performing arts since the mid-20th century. At first, in the age of television, this shift only affected live drama. But with the rise of digital video disks and streaming, it came to affect films as well. Thus, as I am writing, the 'theatre' as a public setting for collective experience is taken to be at perpetual risk of disappearing altogether. Here, it becomes important to recall what has been always seen as distinctive – even provocative – about theatrical presentations from the ancient to the modern eras. When theatre is done well, the actors appear to mean what they say and do on stage, which then elicits a response from the audience as if they were witnesses to – if not participants in – a real event. Whereas Plato believed that such performances were always potentially subversive of the status quo by virtue of arousing thoughts and feelings that could not be easily suppressed once people left the theatre, Aristotle held that the theatre constituted a safe environment for the release of emotions which neutralized any of the performance's subversive potential – provided that the playwright scripted a plot that followed a 'natural order', namely, one where all the loose ends of the action are ultimately resolved.

There are two senses in which academic knowledge lends itself to 'theatrical' presentation in the above sense. The first is that academic knowledge typically starts from premises that challenge whatever might be the default 'common sense' position of the audience. The second is that academic knowledge plays out its counterintuitive premises in considerable detail, ideally so that the audience eventually come to make them their own. Put this way, the academically trained mind would seem to end up inhabiting an alternative reality, which if carried over into 'normal' reality could have jarring, if not explosive, consequences. It was exactly the sort of thing that concerned Plato about dramatic performances, especially good ones that make the script come alive. To be sure, video versions of lectures that can be played, replayed, paused, perhaps even edited, etc. – all at the user's convenience – dilute, if not destroy, much of this effect. Nevertheless, by taking live performances to be the gold standard of education, academia may be able to reverse the value of teaching *vis-à-vis* research so that it looks more like acting *vis-à-vis* scripting.

Interestingly, Max Weber (1958), in his classic defence of academic freedom, which included the freedom of the student to learn, stressed the need for lecturers to refrain from dogmatism to keep options open so that students can decide matters for themselves. Such advice would seem to go against the Aristotelian safeguard that the lecturer should resolve all the loose ends into some kind of balanced package. Instead Weber would license students to leave the classroom thinking that there is still much – if not everything – to play for in pursuing the various strands of counterintuitive reasoning to which they have been just exposed. This is exactly the Humboldtian spirit – at once inspiring and dangerous – that has enabled the classroom to serve as a crucible for the next generation of innovation for the past two centuries.

3 A VATICAN FACE WITH A VEGAS HEART: THE ACADEMIC CAESAR'S POLITICAL ECONOMY

The relative ease with which Americans have been able to apply the financial model of the church to the university is what I mean by the 'Vatican face' of the university in the title of this section. The charge of Humboldt and other state officials has been to try to recreate that sentiment in the public sector, where it is more natural to think of education, like health, as a 'service' whose value rests on how well it enables people to cope with life-chances for which the state is ultimately held responsible. Expressed in most general terms, the practical problem is how to justify a financial regime for universities that does not cause the people funding them to expect most of the benefits to accrue close to the point of service delivery. My solution constitutes the 'Vegas heart' of the university, to which the rest of this section is devoted. Its financial plan is modelled on that of a casino – that is, dedicated to the encouragement of risk-taking.

Evidence for the university's Vegas heart appears initially as budgetary cross-subsidization. This is the time-honoured practice of taking from the rich and giving to the poor academic departments. In the extreme case, the profits generated by the medical school may underwrite philosophy classes with three students. That universities successfully impose overhead costs on external funders partly reflects the legitimacy generally accorded to such cross-subsidization. A university is not simply a marketplace where the various disciplines set up their stalls, but a corporate entity expressly dedicated to the maintenance of all forms of systematic inquiry. Lest we be sentimental, this show of intellectual integrity amounts to a strategy for pooling risk. The underlying economic rationale is that, lacking any long-term correlation between funding research and producing significant knowledge, it is wisest for those lucky enough to have struck rich to underwrite those unlucky enough to have struck poor. After all, fortunes are likely to be, if not reversed, at least levelled, in the future – say, once other medical schools acquire the knowledge that accorded the innovator an initial advantage.

But the Vegas heart of academia is, perhaps unwittingly, shared by society at large. Because universities today are expected to provide skills directly relevant to the increasing number of people who are destined for, in 20th-century parlance, 'white-collar' jobs, it is often forgotten that the state has traditionally regarded universities as public-spirited casinos in which citizens are forced to gamble some proportion of their wealth via tax payments. Until a half- to a quarter-century ago, the vast majority of people whose taxes funded universities had to tell a rather complicated story to justify the investment. Perhaps a relative or friend used academic achievement as a vehicle for personal advancement and upward class mobility. But more likely a complete stranger advanced knowledge in a way that benefited everyone, say, by curing a common disease or expanding our understanding of reality. When such singular 'Einstein' moments occur, people appear willing to excuse all their previous tax expenditure that subsidized the education of people who, for whatever reason, had squandered their opportunity.

This attitude is quite rational under certain economic conditions. The most obvious one is that the investors can benefit as freely as possible from the intellectual windfall. While it took Albert Einstein to come up with the theory of relativity, any of a number of people could have arrived at the theory under the right circumstances, and there was no prior reason to believe that Albert would be that person. To be sure, it might have happened somewhat earlier or later than it did. But if we truly believe that Einstein made a lasting contribution to knowledge (perhaps because he hit upon something deep about the nature of reality), not that he was riding the wave of the latest intellectual fad, then this is how those who subsidized his education should respond. Einstein received his reward upfront as an incentive for him to do something to merit the investment in him, as one of a number of academically trained people. Had Einstein failed to produce the goods, he would not have been penalized, but equally his success does not warrant his receiving *additional* financial benefit. The financial gamble on Einstein was taken not by Einstein himself but the society forced to bet on him (and others) through their taxes because he passed some state-sanctioned academic examinations. Einstein's success is simply grounds for society to continue trusting the state's investment of its taxes, at least in higher education.

Intellectual property law generally accepts that Einstein does not deserve additional remuneration – but for the wrong reasons. Einstein is not entitled to a patent for the theory of relativity, but lawyers say this is because his intellectual work consisted in discovering laws of nature that did not require human effort for their existence and over which no human could thereby exercise ownership. The legal justification harks back to a theologized version of the labour theory of value, whereby human discoveries are essentially acts of copying God's inventions. However, the Vegas heart of the university implies a critique that recalls the most probing examination of the labour theory of value as defended by Karl Marx, its last great champion in economics.

The author was Eugen von Böhm-Bawerk (1851–1914), the late 19th-century Austrian finance minister and Joseph Schumpeter's economics teacher at the University of Vienna. He argued that workers did not deserve a share in the profits gained from their labours because they had been already paid in wages for work whose market value had yet to be determined. Part of the risk that an entrepreneur undertakes is the employment of labour to produce things that perhaps no one will buy. Workers rightly demand fair wages regardless of consumer fickleness. In this respect, Böhm-Bawerk took the labour theory of value more literally than Marx, who, like his Christian predecessors (but unlike Böhm-Bawerk), did not believe that the labour market was a natural guarantor of fair wages. But by the same token, workers are not entitled to additional payment if the products happen to sell. That would turn the entrepreneur's calculated risk into a sure loss, thereby creating a disincentive to industry.

The lesson for universities is clear. The state ministry, board of trustees or senior academic administrators should behave like corporate entrepreneurs who adopt a liberal attitude towards investment but a conservative attitude towards returns. This entails protecting students and staff even when their returns as investments are poor without extravagantly rewarding them when they are good. Thus, student fees and stipends across disciplines should not be excessively influenced by graduates' anticipated incomes, and similarly faculty salaries should not mimic the spread in the demand for different types of knowledge. In short, university finances should not be tightly bound to fluctuating market indicators. After all, the market advantage currently enjoyed by a form of knowledge is bound to erode over time as it comes to be more widely possessed and eventually absorbed into the infrastructure of civilized society. In fact, the university encourages this very erosion as part of the creative destruction of social capital that constitutes the institution's Vatican face.

If a university aims to maintain the lifelong activity of intelligent but fallible beings – a natural rendering of tenured academic appointments – then quickly spotted truth always has the potential to cost the institution more in the long term than belatedly discovered error. This is due to the temptation for academic innovators to become what economists deride as *rent-seekers* – people who discourage subsequent development or application of their original insights by making the entry costs too high for newcomers (cf. McKenzie and Tullock 2012: Part V). To be sure, the ordinary institutionalization of academic disciplines encourages rent-seeking, thereby amplifying 'path-dependency' in the growth of knowledge. What Thomas Kuhn (1970) notoriously called a 'paradigm' is no more than the conversion of an innovator's conceptual framework into an authorized blueprint for further research in a field that could have been – and probably still could be – addressed from a radically different conceptual framework. That paradigms are so marked in intellectual work reflects the halo effect that easily accompanies the initial generation of a few striking research results.

However, again taking the long view of the intellectual speculator, fetishizing priority in research caters to the superstition that the first route into a new field is the only or best route. Of course, if enough people pay long enough lip service to this superstition, it can turn into a self-fulfilling prophecy, at which point it becomes honoured as a 'research tradition' dominated by rituals of pilgrimage and patronage that are very hard to avoid or escape. Thus, a postdoctoral fellowship at the right lab or a letter from the right professor can be the make-or-break moment in a fledgling academic's career.

In 'natural markets' this problem does not arise because the notable success of a new product triggers in the minds of would-be entrepreneurs the prospect of more efficient means of reaching the same, related, or better ends. Novelty serves as an incentive for creative destruction. To be sure, the legal history of capitalism has increasingly put the brakes on this tendency through the extension of intellectual property rights. But as we shall see in the next section, this much decried use of the law to restrict free trade merely follows the lead of academics who mark, if not outright create, their turf by spontaneously generating trademark jargons and tariffs of technique, obeisance to which is paid in the 'literature reviews' and 'citation counts' of journal articles.

Keep in mind that the primary application of 'disciplines' to fields of academic inquiry is a 19th-century development, related to the institutionalization of the Ph.D. as the degree certifying professionalism in academia (Clark 2006). Before that time, 'discipline' was largely used in the context of the religious life (on which Max Weber's 'Science as a Vocation' (1958) continued to draw) and, by the late Middle Ages, to cover the administrative functions of 'doctors' (of medicine, law, theology) who operated in both sacred and secular spheres.

Although academics are inclined to see universities as organized around disciplines, the specialized professional needs and demands of the different disciplines pull the university in competing directions, and the Academic Caesar must be able to stand up to them. In particular, the natural sciences have increasingly strained the university's internal cohesion and 'team-spiritedness', given their high capital investment needs, closely tied to the highly technical character of their work, as well as their intensely competitive culture and proneness to veer into politically and ethically sensitive ground. To create equity among disciplines whose resource requirements and prospective achievements vary so widely, the Academic Caesar may need to reopen the issues that Immanuel Kant originally raised in his polemical 1798 essay, *The Contest of the Faculties*, a major inspiration for the Humboldtian University (Fuller 2013b).

In a nutshell, the Academic Caesar should be able to counteract academics' propensities to pump needless ontological gas into the words and practices they happened to have found useful in advancing the course of inquiry. Recalling the law's historic role as the nemesis of monopoly capitalism in the US Progressive Era, we might say that the university functions here as an 'epistemic trust-buster'. There are two general ways of thinking about this function, both of which are designed to counteract specifically discipline-based assessment bodies (i.e. public and private professional accrediting agencies) that exist independently of the universities, but whose members they are deemed qualified to judge. Incentives need to be offered for academics, on the one hand, to self-deconstruct their epistemic privilege by translating their research into teaching, and on the other hand, to vacate their field of research in favour of another. Of course, there are no guarantees that these institutionally induced career shifts will lead to new insights. But that is part of the exhilaration of being a member of the 'creative class': it is less a matter whether you win or lose than that you enjoy an opportunity to play a game of *potentially* major social significance – the happy face of 'casino capitalism' (Florida 2002).

4 THE ACADEMIC CAESAR'S BIGGEST ENEMY: RENTIER CAPITALISM

Understood as features of the natural history of humanity (i.e. not necessarily in their normatively desirable forms), capitalism and academia can each be understood as one long path-dependent pattern recognition exercise, the periodic results of which have generative powers: patents and paradigms, respectively. This turn of mind is common to the capitalist, who is driven into ever more speculative realms ('futures') to generate profits, and the academic, at least in the modern sense of 'scientist' who seeks ever higher orders of unity and control (aka 'knowledge and power'). What one calls 'finance', the other calls 'theory'.

In both cases, the process begins the same. You observe some successful yet amorphously defined interaction – perhaps one in which you are a participant – under a variety of conditions, but without knowing exactly what makes the interaction work. Nevertheless, you are sure that it is neither arbitrary nor simply reducible to 'habit'. You then 'capitalize' on this observation by proposing a more abstract version of the interaction that can be applied regularly, say, through instruction or codification. If you are successful, you will have generated knowledge of those interactions as what Marxists call 'surplus value' and philosophers of mind call 'supervenience', in that the new knowledge goes beyond that of the original parties to the interactions yet it would not have been possible without them. (An interesting point of reference is Sohn-Rethel 1978.)

Intellectual property law was designed for this way of thinking of things. The patent is an abstraction from specific physical or human interactions whereby the original moving parts, or agents, are turned into placeholders for bringing about the same effects in various ways, as prescribed in the patent. Ideally, at least from the inventor's standpoint, a patent specifies what mathematicians call a 'function' (Fuller 2010b, 2013a). In the terms of US pragmatist philosopher Charles Sanders Peirce, it is the product of an 'abductive' inference rendered mechanical: A template for structuring action has been generated. From the law's standpoint, this is an attractor for rents, or 'royalties', as others see the utility of applying the patent for their own purposes. Indeed, a well-designed patent generates a 'domain of application' into which the patent-holder might then expand with still further inventions or over which it might simply exert territorial control, again in the form of rents.

Something similar happens in the case of more strictly academic innovations that do not involve technological invention. The process here, though less formally enforced, is facilitated by the academic referencing system, which fosters relations of dependency among authors around a highly cited text (Fuller 1997: chap. 4, Fuller 2000a: chap. 5). Such a text, a paradigm for further research, effectively 'sublimates' the details of specifically situated activities into an abstractly worded version that may be easily imported by others for use and development. This appropriation is subject to a payment of tribute – another form of rent – the giving of 'credit', on which the academic citation culture is based. This is the currency in which careers are nowadays made or broken. Thus, the administrative exhortation for academics to publish highly cited articles in high-impact journals would end up turning academics into intellectual property developers in the high-rent end of their disciplines.

However, real estate development in academia is a many-splendored thing. In sociology, two rather contrary attitudes co-exist. On the one hand, the ethnomethodologist Wes Sharrock (1974) has argued that academics own the knowledge that they produce in collaboration with subjects, who are provided with a contract concerning the terms of engagement. Thus, they might be paid for their cognitive labour and assured that they will not be exposed to harm or degradation, but they forfeit the right to exercise control over the disposition of the resulting knowledge product. This is very much in line with a capitalist view of knowledge production. Of course, as a matter of courtesy, the sociologist might ask the subjects to opine on how their input has been contextualized. But in the end, the sociologist is sovereign over how such opinions are taken. In contrast, a less sectarian ethnographer, Michael Burawoy (2005), would reverse the relation of ownership, at least as a normative benchmark. He believes that sociologists have a prima facie obligation to amplify the voice of the relatively voiceless in society. This would seem to imply that the sociologist is 'owned' by these subordinate groups in the manner of a lawyer who serves as an advocate for a client. Both are constrained with regard to representation, since the ultimate goal in both cases is to a positive outcome for the client/subject.

In both the more strictly capitalist and the academic cases, the knowledge gained has been 'commodified' in the word's original Latin sense of occupying a certain (conceptual) space that needs to be negotiated by anyone wishing to navigate over a more general terrain (Fuller 2010b). Take oil's centrality as a source of energy. Commodified oil differs from actual petrol in that the former's value – set in a commodities market – is determined by the importance of petrol's contribution to various vital human processes and what it would cost to replace it in the various cases. The commodities market deals with oil as a projected aggregate matter, not as it is currently experienced by particular producers and consumers of petrol at, say, the gas pump. Nevertheless, given the interlocking nature of markets, the commodities market price of petrol eventually affects the price at the pump.

However, what keeps capitalism dynamic – at least in theory – is that this situation is seen as providing opportunities to invent ways of, say, opening up more oil reserves or even developing alternative energy sources. These moves, the sources of entrepreneurial innovation, are less obviously present in academia. Its general mind-set and incentive structure are not right for it. Academics are normally more about 'standing on the shoulders of giants' than figuring out more efficient ways of getting to the top. Even such a staple academic practice as 'critique' is ultimately about delimiting the validity or applicability of a knowledge claim in order to make room for one's own or some other perspective that occupies space which the original knowledge claim does not.

Knowledge *replacement* in the proper sense, when it does happen in academia, typically takes place through attrition, as works simply stop being discussed or cited. It is rare to find the equivalent of the 'creative destruction' of academic markets. This would be tantamount to an openly declared 'scientific revolution', which deliberately sets out to reorganize an entire field of inquiry – and succeeds by consigning the previous regime to the dustbin of history. Antoine Lavoisier's self-declared 'chemical revolution' in the late 18th century may still be the clearest case in point, as most of the other great scientific revolutions were declared only in retrospect by historians and journalists (Cohen 1985).

But it would be a mistake to think that academics inherently lack the resources to engage in creative destruction. In fact, were teaching understood as the publicly performed deconstruction of research, then the creative destruction of knowledge claims would be happening on a regular basis in the classroom. In practice, this would mean that students would demonstrate mastery of course materials by literally putting matters 'in their own terms', which is to say, in a language with which they are most comfortable yet captures the essence of what they were supposed to have learned. Their model would be the instructor's own relatively informal and accessible manner when discussing the assigned course materials. I alluded to this pedagogical policy towards the end of the Introduction, when discussing the palpable 'added value' of a university education to students.

Unfortunately, teachers too often want students to learn to decode academic texts simply in order to reproduce that very code in their own texts, which involves paying appropriate tribute to previous keepers of the code. Over-scripted PowerPoint presentations add to this effect. Either in the classroom or the conference, academics too often appear like bad actors mouthing scripts written by someone else. The attentive audience member – student or colleague – yearns for a more capacious actor who could make the script their own. This would be akin to 'method acting', which taps into the actor's own cognitive-emotional hinterland (Benedetti 2004: chap. 4). In the academic context, this hinterland could be productively mined in the question-and-answer period. Unfortunately, this period is normally filled by academics ring-fencing their knowledge claims, so that little more than artful repetition passes for a response. Under the circumstances, one cannot blame university authorities for thinking that PowerPoints and other products of academic labour are more suitable candidates for legal protection than in the labouring academics themselves.

Unsurprisingly, then, much – if not most – of the evaluation of student performance occurs at the level of the competent handling of sources. After all, this is how academics accord value to themselves, a practice which university administrators merely take advantage of. Even positive professional peer-review judgements – say, 'a useful addition to the literature' – tend to stress the essentially reproductive character of normal academic research, in which one's own work is a well-defined incremental change in the same basic direction. Thus, *plagiarism* looms large as a crime against scholarship – as if correctly estimating one's own contribution to meritorious work were more important than the work itself.

Yet, at the same time, more thoughtful scholars do not rate highly either students or scholars whose playing by the rules results in knowledge claims so heavily dependent on properly acknowledged sources that their pieces could have been generated by a computer programmed with the set of relevant references as input data. Unfortunately, much of what passes for academic work in our era of mass publishing has exactly this character. Such works sit closer to a kind of 'plagiarism' that is worth worrying about: call it *Plagiarism Plus,* the sort of thing that Kuhn (1970) euphemistically termed 'normal science'. In learning to reference academic sources properly, students become able both to communicate in a way that their scholarly audience will easily understand and to think about academic work as intellectual property which they can rent for their own purposes through proper citation. However, the connection between mastery of these skills and mastery of a domain of scholarship is by no means obvious. I am not the only reader of well-placed sociology journal articles who often wonders whether an author has understood the impressive list of cited works, given the deployment of the works in the author's text. And of course, Alan Sokal managed to ignite the 'science wars' precisely on this premise with his well-placed 'hoax' article in a leading US cultural studies journal (Ross 1996).

In fetishizing plagiarism, academic culture reveals its proclivity to rentier capitalism. Although the proscription against plagiarism tends to be presented as a defence of authorial originality, in fact it amounts to a protection of intellectual property. The result is significant value confusion, which has arguably sown the seeds of its own destruction. The dialectical logic is as follows. Originality is cashed out as the 'hard graft' of mastering the 'craft of scholarship', which cannot be simulated through the stylistically inept cut-and-paste jobs that have typically passed for plagiarized work. But of course, plagiarists then raise their game, and in the process approximate – still by more economical means – the very skills that the 'true' scholars possess. Thus, in the case of these 'improved' plagiarists, their sources are quite diverse, appropriated with some judgement, and executed in a way that papers over more glaring stylistic differences among the original texts. This has spurred the development of computer-based programs such as 'Turnitin', which survey all internet-based data sources for textual overlap, which in turn has spawned student-oriented programs to ensure their papers are in the 'safe zone'. And so, the game of 'cat and mouse' continues to ever greater degrees of sophistication. In the process, students unwittingly refine their scholarly skills, etc.

The arts have a much healthier attitude to fraud, be it plagiarism or its complement, forgery (cf. Fuller 2007b: chap. 5). If an experienced practitioner or connoisseur cannot spot the fraud, then the artist gets away with it – though there will always be opportunities for future critics and scholars to return to the 'scene of the crime', so to speak. Indeed, the greater public visibility and notoriety enjoyed by the artwork, something which every true artist desires, the more vulnerable it becomes to this treatment. (It is thus easy to see why the great art historian Ernst Gombrich was a fan of Karl Popper.) Indeed, return visits to an artist's sources have sometimes served to shift artistic reputations, as people come to realize that an apparent 'original' really got all his or her best ideas from people who had gone unnoticed at the time. But sometimes even this additional knowledge does not seem to matter much. The artist's reputation remains intact – if only because of the cleverness with which the artist papered over the cracks between the borrowings. Indeed, this may well be the 'art' of the artist. Harold Bloom (1973) crafted an interesting psychoanalytic account of artistic creativity on the back of this point under the rubric of 'the anxiety of influence'.

It is too bad that academia does not adopt this relatively relaxed attitude to plagiarism and fraud, which would effectively leave the uncaught student to dwell productively in his or her guilt. In contrast, our current practices draw attention to just how much academics feel the need to protect their turf from unworthy interlopers. Yet, what is the source of this need? Perhaps academics feel that their insights are so hard won, so naturally scarce, that someone who simply steals them or makes them up whole cloth is doing an injustice to the sense of labour implied by genuine academic achievement. Artists do not generally have this hang-up. Rightly or wrongly, they believe that they are full of ideas and the real challenge is to harness them together in some coherent 'work'. Artists often know the source of their most productive ideas, but they do not feel the need to assign credit. This is for two quite sensible reasons: (1) under a slight change of circumstances, they might have got those very same ideas from other heads, including their own; (2) the artwork that they create from those sources will speak for itself by doing something significant that the source works did not do. Once again, the intended publicity of the artwork ultimately puts both propositions to the test.

Meanwhile, back on Planet Academia, we continue to live in a world where ideas are scarce, not abundant, and their value is judged in terms of who made them rather than what is made of them. Thus, we fail to appreciate that the most devious forgers of original work will have mastered the skills that we would have demanded of them. The key difference is that the forger treats 'the archive' (aka 'the internet' for today's generation) as an extended memory store, not as something ontologically distinct from his or her own being. In more formal disciplines, where the scope for epistemic innovation amounts to little more than technical sophistication, there is a dawning awareness of both the pervasiveness of unacknowledged intellectual influence and the futility of trying to bring anyone to justice for it. Analytic philosophy provides a ready supply of cases in point, perhaps the most notorious of which ironically involves the origins of the 'causal theory of reference' (Humphreys and Fetzer 1998).

My aim in all this is not to repackage a crisis of ego identity ('boundary issues') as some higher epistemic virtue, or even claim that we are already the extensions of some grand epistemic 'borg' (though there may be some truth to that). Rather, I am asserting an unconditional right of someone who has been allowed into society's official epistemic sphere as a 'student' to range freely within it, understood as a 'commons', unless specifically stopped by a relevant authority. In short, the burden should be placed on academics to demonstrate epistemic trespass among those whom they have already admitted as their potential equals. Moreover, these demonstrations would be cast more in aesthetic than moral terms. In that case, the problem with detected plagiarism is more that it is detected than that it is plagiarized: it was not good enough to pass as original. Statistically speaking, a confident academic culture would prefer an examination regime that ends up with 'false negatives' than 'false positives' in matters of fraud. After all, a teacher fooled is a student learned.

5 THE ACADEMIC CAESAR'S ULTIMATE TASK: THE MANUFACTURE OF KNOWLEDGE AS A SECOND-ORDER GOOD

The historically surest strategy for universities to maintain their autonomy in a relatively unregulated knowledge market has been to shift from producing knowledge as a first-order to a second-order good (Fuller 2000a: chap. 6). This was the context in which the analytic philosopher Quine (1960) spoke of 'semantic ascent', which is more colloquially known as 'going meta'. Earlier in this chapter I mentioned the centrality of Kant's *The Contest of the Faculties* to Humboldt's idea of the modern university. For Kant, philosophy – a field which heretofore lacked a clear academic identity – provided the crucible for forging such second-order goods by promising a common standard for evaluating knowledge claims and hence adjudicating among the contesting faculties. In the 20th century the search for this standard came to be the commonly accepted meaning of 'epistemology'.

Before turning to a more general institutional strategy for ensuring that the university corners the market on knowledge as a second-order good, it is worth highlighting three distinct discipline-based strategies for achieving largely the same effect:

1 The academic projects a speculative theory or perhaps even a realm of abstract objects, which effectively grants a prospecting right, such that anyone who later empirically validates or instantiates aspects of the projection is effectively forced to pay some sort of tribute to the prospector. Mathematics retains its high academic standing on this basis, given its track record of anticipating deep configurations of reality, ranging from symbolic logic to non-Euclidean geometry.

2 The academic – typically a humanist – identifies a precursor individual or culture on whose behalf a retrospective entitlement claim is made, either positively or negatively. For example, one might claim that a characteristically Western knowledge claim in fact was developed by non-Westerners or, alternatively, that an allegedly universal knowledge claim only enjoys that status by virtue of having been maintained by Western authorities (implying that other potentially legitimate non-Western claims are being suppressed).

3 The academic – typically in a public policy context – is concerned that an entire area of research may remain unfunded because of its lack of short-term policy relevance. The remedy then is a version of Pascal's Wager, which attempts to blackmail people into belief in God by having them consider the consequences of unbelief in a world where God does turn out to exist. In other words, even if someone doesn't see the immediate benefit of your research, make the case for the potential harm if it is neglected. Thus, second-order knowledge goods are generated as a form of higher-order insurance. Research into areas as diverse as the global ecology (to prevent massive climate change) and artificial intelligence (to prevent 'superintelligent' machines) would fall under this rubric.

But suppose we take the idea of knowledge as a 'second-order good' as a more literally economic conception. In this case, 'autonomy' implies an ability to turn the market to one's own advantage, so that rival knowledge producers are forced to compete on one's preferred turf. This is another way to look at Schumpeter's (1934) original definition of entrepreneurship as the 'creative destruction' of markets. Henry Ford was Schumpeter's exemplary entrepreneur because he reconfigured the transport market so that his own product, the automobile, set the standard that rivals then had to meet or surpass. Not only today, but throughout their history, universities have periodically had to 'creatively destroy' knowledge markets in order to overcome challenges to their prime position as authoritative knowledge producers.

At first, the relevance of the Schumpeterian entrepreneur to today's aspiring Academic Caesar may not seem so clear. After all, Ford actually produced a first-order innovation on the basis of which he generated a new market standard, which became the second-order innovation. But on closer inspection, universities prove not to be so different. Take the matter of accrediting primary and secondary schools, both in terms of courses taught and people licensed to teach them. Although universities do not exert much control over day-to-day school practices, nevertheless they have played a major role in defining the foundations and even the logic of instruction of the various taught subjects, which to a large extent mirror those taught in universities. For example, in the UK, geography is one of the few subjects whose place in the school curriculum was *not* due to university-based initiatives (Goodson 1988: 160–96). Little surprise, then, that the proportion of university-bound high school graduates is routinely treated as the gold standard of school performance precisely because academia is presumed to be the primary determinant of what schools teach.

Today this last point seems perfectly reasonable, especially given the increasing percentage of each student cohort attending university. However, a generation ago, when university attendance – outside the United States – was half its current cohort rate, the career trajectories of high school graduates and academic degree-holders were much more distinct. Yet even then universities were setting the standard of school performance. In this context, the relevant first-order goods manufactured by universities have been discipline-based textbooks, simplified versions of which continue to make their way into high school classes, with the overall effect of standardizing how teachers communicate their subject areas.

To be sure, if the expectation of university attendance by high school graduates continues, then Academic Caesars may be compelled to cultivate a less condescending attitude towards secondary and even primary schools when defining the knowledge content of taught subject areas. In particular, schoolteachers tend to be more sensitive to non-academic – notably ethnic- and religious-based – sources of epistemic authority that students bring from their local environments. In the past, state enforcement of secular education was specifically designed to counter such potential obstacles to national solidarity. Indeed, the disciplinary identity of sociology in the early 20th century, especially in France and the US, was tied to this project of harmonizing epistemic standards across the entire education system, one which US Progressives such as John Dewey specifically identified as the nation's 'melting pot'.

However, as universities lose the state's unconditional political and economic support, they will need to negotiate anew their relationship to the local knowledges that are most naturally given voice at the school level. While the struggle between universities and schools over what knowledge is worth teaching is bound to intensify in the coming years, at least the contesting parties share a common understanding of knowledge as a second-order good, namely, a potentially universal standard of thought and conduct.

A much more serious threat to the university autonomy is posed by knowledge managers who call into question the very existence of knowledge as a second-order good, over which universities might lay *prima facie* claim. Here we need to keep in mind that currently popular phrases for our times, such as 'knowledge society' and 'knowledge economy', mainly refer to the opening up of the market for knowledge goods to new suppliers (Fuller 2002: chap. 1). As a result of this cardinal moment in the shift towards a neo-liberal political economy, universities were forced not only to spread their resources more thinly, but also to confront the sorts of internal tensions that an Academic Caesar normally sublimates. After all, institutes devoted purely to research, such as corporate laboratories in the past and today's science parks, have operated with fewer encumbrances than universities in need of maintaining a delicate balance between several constituencies: research peers at other universities, campus colleagues from other disciplines, as well as the university's own dedicated review boards to matters of ethics and finance. Similarly, a training centre with reliable access to relevant employers can function more efficiently – at least from the standpoint of student *qua* consumer – than degree programmes that subordinate job training to a systematic presentation of the body of knowledge represented by an academic discipline.

Under the circumstances, it is easy to draw the knowledge manager's conclusion that the university has become an obsolete organization that tries to do too many things at once and hence does them all sub-optimally (cf. Fuller 2002: chap. 4). In this context, the university's longevity is used to count against its future prospects: the institution has simply become entrenched in its old ways, which renders it incapable of adapting to today's changing market environment. The obvious solution would seem to be to disaggregate the university's functions into organizations focused primarily on either the research or teaching markets. However, this would be the wrong conclusion, if history is our guide.

The successful strategy for university reinvention emerged in the mid-19th century when Oxford and Cambridge, already over 600 years old, had yet to house scientific laboratories on their grounds, even though major industrial innovation was increasingly tied to research conducted in such facilities and, in any case, had already occurred in factory settings for at least a century. While Oxbridge of course eventually allowed the construction of labs on their grounds, their principal response to this challenge was inspired by the theologian who coined the word 'scientist' in English, William Whewell, who is nowadays seen as the founder of the historical and philosophical study of science.

Whewell proposed something that we now take for granted: namely, that inventions may emerge in all sorts of non-academic settings but only academics can determine whether these inventions are anything more than lucky accidents. This is because academics – unlike inventors – are devoted to making sure that all of what we know hangs together as a systematic unity, something that is regularly performed in the curriculum as new knowledge is integrated into existing conceptual frameworks to inform the next generation. In that case, for any invention, the academic wants to know why it works when it does, and especially when it does not work, which in turn provides grounds for improvement – ideally in the disciplined setting of a university laboratory.

In this context, Oxbridge could convert its perceived liabilities into virtues: namely, its ideological basis in Anglican theology and its material basis in property ownership. Together they provided grounds sufficiently removed from the mental and physical spaces of industrial innovation to make Oxbridge appear honest brokers of knowledge claims emanating from those sites. Moreover, in positioning Oxbridge as gatekeepers in the otherwise free flow of inventions, Whewell had no intention of stifling that flow. On the contrary, the more disparate the sources of innovation, the more obvious becomes the need to establish common standards for discriminating reliable from unreliable inventions along a variety of dimensions that include not only their theoretical bases – issues that might also concern the government patent office – but also the potential financial and health risks they posed to adopters of the innovations.

It is easy nowadays to overlook the centrality of universities in the institutionalization of standards of empirical reliability in the manufacture and circulation of knowledge products – what managers call 'quality control' and philosophers of science dignify as the 'context of justification' (Fuller 2000a: chap. 6). This development, which explains the strong presence of academics in government regulatory agencies in the 20th century, was at first strongly resisted in legal and business circles as being against the spirit of a liberal society, in which people should be free to assume their own risks (Turner 2003: chap. 5). This strong market sensibility supposed that as long as information about the consequences of adopting an innovation was widely disseminated, anyone capable of participating in public life was mentally equipped to decide for themselves if they should adopt, extend or simply avoid and ignore the innovation.

From this standpoint, the idea that universities should normatively mediate society's knowledge flow appeared to be a thinly veiled attempt to reinvent a modern version of clerical oversight on secular affairs. Instead of the Church sanctifying the King's acts, the university lab would now perform that role for politics and business. Here one might track the pejorative use of the term 'clerisy' for the testimony of 'expert witnesses' in matters of legal import, an image first cultivated in early 20th-century America by Hugo Münsterberg, whom William James had hired to run Harvard's psychology laboratory (Winter 2012: chap. 1). Nevertheless, to classical liberals who remained suspicious of any barriers to free trade, demands that new products pass tests of 'validity' and 'reliability' constructed in academic settings prior to market exposure smacked of what we earlier noted as 'rent-seeking', that is, a cost tied exclusively to the ownership, rather than the productive use, of capital – in this case, the cultural capital that comes from simply being the keeper of epistemic standards, on which everyone must rely. So, how do universities manage to retain their market advantage by providing the sort of second-order knowledge goods associated with quality control standards?

The answer is that universities systematically counter society's centrifugal tendencies with their own centripetal ones. In other words, as society's capacity to alter its knowledge base increases, the threat of fragmentation – indeed, the loss of society's collective memory – also increases. Imagine the character of knowledge in today's society, if our proverbial knowledge manager got his way and the university's functions were disaggregated to teaching-only and research-only organizations. The former would be exclusively oriented towards the labour market, namely, the efficient provision of job-related skills. The latter would be exclusively oriented to a variety of clients for whom new knowledge can increase the value of their goods. The one sort of activity would embed knowledge in people and the other in products, but over time it would be difficult to see what qualifies both activities as oriented towards 'knowledge' *per se*. At that point, knowledge would become segmented into two discrete markets, one for *techniques* (i.e. embodied in the person) and another for *technologies* (i.e. embodied outside the person). The idea of knowledge as the unifying and universalizing mode of inquiry epitomized in Max Weber's (1958) resonant phrase, 'Science as a vocation', would have disappeared. So too would society's sense of self-consciousness. It is rescue from this 'postmodern' condition that ultimately justifies the existence of the Academic Caesar.

In conclusion, let us consider the broader political horizons into which Academic Caesarism plays in terms of a historical precedent for the journey ahead. The university today is being forced to return to its roots in the development of medieval city-states as 'corporations'. Like the original scholastics, today's academics need to defend their autonomy in the face of various extramural forces that make claims on its activities. In the Middle Ages, the city-states constructed walls, which led to their being known as 'communes' (i.e. 'walled together' in Latin). Originally this was a matter of self-protection, a theme which Sassower (2000) updates in terms of 'academia as asylum'. However, the self-protective character of the original communes eventually became a source of strength. Think of it this way: people of recognized material or intellectual wealth – the etymology of 'talent' captures both – would be easy prey in the lawless world, but if they can develop their wealth in relative isolation, then eventually they would be able to provide a greater benefit to those outside its walls. In this context, 'freedom' is seen not as a condition to avoid utility altogether but to prepare for providing greater utility. This helps to explain the seclusion and often secrecy that has characterized both academic and guild life – and was secularized in the modern era in intellectual property law.

Underwriting this line of argument is a logic of incubation, the sort of extended gestation which Plato originally thought was necessary for the production of philosopher-kings and which Locke declared to be characteristic of *Homo sapiens* as a species. Historically, the medieval city-states were organized by people with the wherewithal to create the requisite autonomous space without getting involved in the 'Investiture Controversy' of the 11th and 12th centuries, when the papacy and the princes routinely contested the appointment of local prelates. Until the Concordat of Worms in 1122, jurisdictional boundaries were so ambiguous that one's life could be in jeopardy by being aligned with the wrong parties. To be sure, issues of this sort have not disappeared, but they were effectively normalized with the emergence of the 'corporations', social entities possessing the rights of 'artificial persons' with an inherent 'right to incubation', so to speak, even in the face of a resistant environment. Modern legacies of this medieval legal innovation include not only the inviolate individual, nation-state and the business firm, but also the university. For anyone aspiring to the title of 'Academic Caesar', the maintenance of this sense of ontological boundary is ultimately the core business.

2

PEER REVIEW: KEY TO KNOWLEDGE AS A PUBLIC GOOD OR THE ACADEMIC GUILD'S LAST STAND?

1 INTRODUCTION AND OVERVIEW OF THE ARGUMENT

Peer review is an easy – and to a large extent justified – target for cynicism on the part of both aspiring Academic Caesars and neo-liberal policymakers. To be sure, most non-academics encounter 'peer review' as a quality control signal in knowledge production. However, for the academics themselves, it can feel like an exquisite combination of blackmail and extortion. On the blackmail side, academics wishing to publish in a certain field know in advance that they have no chance of acceptance unless their work formally acknowledges the work of a specific range of researchers. On the extortion side, academics who have undergone peer review may be told that a condition of publication is not simply to address clear errors and inadequacies but in addition to incorporate considerations of specific interest to the reviewer, which under normal circumstances would be regarded as a needless burden.

Nevertheless, amid the variously lodged calls for academic inquiry to be more 'open sourced' and 'publicly oriented', it has been common for both supporters and opponents of the neo-liberal 'mode 2' knowledge production to agree on the inviolability of 'peer review' as a core academic value. Indeed, nowadays the tendency especially among the critics of neo-liberalism is to portray peer review, under the guise of 'mutual accountability', as a mark of solidarity and collective resistance against larger forces in the political economy that threaten to compromise academic freedom (Boden and Epstein 2011). From the standpoint pursued in this chapter, such an overestimation of peer review may be

seen as sounding the death rattle of the academic guild mentality. As a matter of fact, the value of peer review in the larger political economy of knowledge production is rather circumscribed and typically conservative in effect. Insofar as peer review can be harnessed to some sort of progressive ends in the neo-liberal academy, it should be in full cognizance of its limitations.

Peer review serves both an epistemic and a moral function, which are quite distinct but easily confused in ways that mystify its significance in academic inquiry – or 'science', in the broad *wissenschaftlich* sense. *Epistemically*, peer review 'validates' in the sense of granting a licence to a scientist to draw on a discipline's body of knowledge to advance her own knowledge claims. *Ethically*, peer review signals to the larger public the discipline's trust that the scientist did what she claims to have done. Thus, fraud is seen as the biggest offence against the peer review process. Nevertheless, the history of science reveals that fraud has a complicated – sometimes quite positive – relationship to the advancement of knowledge.

There is an equally complicated relationship between the classical sociological model of peer review – namely, the self-organizing Royal Society – and the advancement of knowledge. In particular, this model works better for retrospective than prospective epistemic judgements. It is easier to tell whether new research carries on than breaks with old research. Not surprisingly, journalists (and suspicious scientists) see groupthink lying behind peer review judgements. Interestingly, commercial publishers – always on the lookout for new markets – are generally motivated to find new domains of knowledge that break peer review monopolies. In short, peer review works very well as a definer of a discipline's mainstream and frontier – but less so as a medium for disposing of particular pieces of research. In conclusion, I suggest how the Academic Caesar might incorporate both the entrepreneurial instinct of publishers and the enlightenment instinct of academics in complementary forms of 'creative destruction' of knowledge markets. My argument accepts much of the logic of neo-liberalism but in a way designed to shore up the distinctiveness of the university as an epistemic institution.

2 IS PEER REVIEW ABOUT THE EPISTEMICS OR THE ETHICS OF SCIENCE?

A philosophically flattering way of defining the function of peer review in the knowledge system is as the means by which research, regardless of origin, comes to be incorporated within a collective body of knowledge, typically an academic discipline. Thus, in the jargon of the philosophy of science, peer review marks the point at which the 'context of justification' takes over from the 'context of discovery'. Idiosyncrasies relating to the discovery process are ironed out or ignored in the peer-reviewed publication, such that readers with the requisite background knowledge and skills – but not intimate knowledge of the author – can build upon the research in question. This helps to explain the specifically *epistemic* premium placed on the 'blindness' of the peer review process – in particular, the reviewers' blindness to the author's identity. More than simply a matter of 'fairness' in the ordinary ethical sense, the ideal reader of a peer-reviewed publication is concerned exclusively with the explicit knowledge claims, the content of which (including their larger contextualization in the literature) could have been made by any relevantly competent inquirer.

In that case, peer review literally *validates* the research in question. I say 'literally' because we need to think of this process in the spirit of the original sense of 'validation', which lingers in the idea of 'valid legal tender' in banking. When a journal publishes a peer-reviewed article, it does not claim that the article is true, but rather that it draws on a common stock of knowledge by appropriate methods to draw conclusions that aim to preserve and, if possible, increase that stock. This is basically a concrete way of stating what 'validity' means in logic. In enforcing peer review, the journal's primary concern is to ensure that the common stock of knowledge that it claims as its own is, whenever possible, enhanced but certainly not debased. In this context, 'deduction' names a safe and 'induction' a risky epistemic investment in that stock. Again, placed in a philosophically flattering light, the peer review process insures against the risk of induction that accompanies all genuinely new knowledge by requiring that authors embed their research in larger, mutually reinforcing theoretical and methodological frameworks from which an author's specific contribution can be (more or less) deduced as the logical next step of this (manufactured) collective investigation.

Nevertheless, *prima facie* most peer-reviewed publications end up yielding little palpable 'added value' for the disciplines to which they purport to contribute. The average article is rarely cited by later publications or, if cited, it is often to highlight its shortcomings. In the next chapter, we shall look on the bright side of this phenomenon and argue that all of this unread literature constitutes a stock of 'undiscovered public knowledge', an epistemic potential waiting to be exploited by public or private bodies willing to fund scholars to resurrect work that had originally fallen stillborn from the presses, to recall David Hume's memorable account of his first book's reception. Indeed, one might metaphysically dignify this 'data mining' task by referring to Karl Popper's (1972) 'third world' of objective knowledge that is an ongoing by-product of human attempts to impose intelligent design on matter – effectively, a 'rolling news feed' from the ontological frontline. Popper's paradigm case of this third world was the realm of mathematical objects, which were generated from second-order reflection on our counting and measuring practices. Were Popper not such a sworn enemy of Hegel, one might call this process 'dialectical'.

But ultimately, peer review is less concerned with the epistemic than the moral justification of the research that is published. The true enemy of the peer review process is *fraud*, the false pretence of having carried out the research that the journal's peers have credited the author through publication. Fraud is tantamount to depositing forged currency in a bank that is then circulated through the economy, contaminating all subsequent business transactions. Thus, it is claimed that fraud that goes undetected until only much later may have catastrophic consequences for the entire body of authorized knowledge. However, counterbalancing these fears is a touching faith in the policing powers of peer review. Both philosophers and sociologists tend to believe that the scientific knowledge system has a remarkable capacity for self-correction, such that the relative rarity of detected fraud corresponds to a genuine lack of frequency in the occurrence of fraud rather than simply a lack of incentive to detect it.

In this context, the concept of 'trust' can be made to do heroic work to justify the relationship between a journal's peer reviewers and authors seeking publication: a classic case of the absence of evidence being taken as evidence for absence – in this case, of fraud. Under normal circumstances, such an inference would be dismissed as fallacious – but in science, it is simply miraculous. This strange combination of scientists being both fearful of fraud and confident in its detection was epitomized in the 1 June 1990 issue of the leading US general science magazine, *Science*, which reported a resolution passed by the governing board of the American Association for the Advancement of Science calling for the US government to grant peer-reviewed journals immunity from prosecution if they display due diligence in catching and reporting fraud in their pages. The proposal went nowhere, but it was meant to perpetuate the idea that the welfare of the public was at risk through the unscrupulous reporting of scientific research – and, conversely, that peer review provided adequate insurance against that risk.

But to what extent are such claims true – or even relevant to the issue of 'fraud'? After all, fraud commits the sin of misrepresentation, a moral not an epistemic fault. Thus, the *Science* editorial attempted to read the undoubted cleverness of the elusive scientific fraudster as a manifestation of unspeakable evil. Nevertheless, the content of a fraudulent piece of work – be it bullshit or plagiarism – may correspond to how the world is, albeit it would take someone else's work to make the case properly: in the case of plagiarism, that work has been already done but has gone unrecognized; in the case of bullshit, that work will be eventually done and the 'fraud' may come to be seen as its anticipation (Fuller 2009: chap. 4). Indeed, the bullshit side of the argument has been quite significant in the history of science, with Galileo and Mendel being just two of the most adept data massagers, if not outright fabricators, who made important knowledge claims that turned out to be largely true but very likely were not quite within their epistemic reach (Fuller 2007b: chap. 5).

Of course, it is somewhat – but only somewhat – anachronistic to attribute 'research fraud' to scientists who lived long before the phrase acquired a clear legal definition. I say 'only somewhat' because sufficient doubts were attached to Galileo's and Mendel's research findings to lead others to shun or persecute them in their own lifetimes. As it turned out, each suffered only a relative short-term loss of status, though that period did extend beyond their lifetimes. Though no one would dare raise the prospect now, a similar vindication may lie in store for Hwang Woo-Suk, the once celebrated South Korean biotechnologist (pictured on the cover of *Time* magazine in 2004) who falsely claimed to have cloned human embryonic stem cells. As the controversy over his actions unfolded, greater emphasis was placed on his failure to follow globally agreed ethical guidelines for securing consent from subjects – egg donations, in this case – than whether it might be possible to clone human stem cells by techniques like those that he claimed to have used. Faith in that latter possibility inspired hundreds of South Korean women to donate their eggs in solidarity with Hwang, even after he was indicted for fraud. A decade later, Hwang remains in the cloning business, reportedly teaming up with a Chinese company to clone 100,000 cattle per year (Clover and Cookson 2015).

In the cases of unscrupulously reported research past and present, it has never been shown that the public welfare was at risk – at least any more so than from actions taken on the back of scrupulously reported research. Nevertheless, the willingness of scientists to associate non-peer-reviewed research and risk to public welfare goes unabated. A cautionary tale in this vein concerns the fate of the UK-based journal *Medical Hypotheses*. As the title suggests, this periodical is devoted to intellectually interesting but untested speculations in the biomedical sciences. Inspired by the solid state physicist and theorist of 'post-academic science', John Ziman, the journal was founded by the maverick physiologist David Horrobin in 1975 specifically to provide a safe haven for what he called 'revolutionary science', which by definition would be rejected by ordinary peer review.

Horrobin took all editorial decisions himself, with occasional consultation of an advisory board. A piece would be published simply on the basis of its logical coherence and scientific plausibility. The paper would not need to present any original research, nor would it need to be compatible with the dominant tendencies in the relevant fields. In regular editorials, Horrobin took aim at the peer review practices of other journals, as well as the use of random critical trials and animal-based experiments in biomedical research. He also promoted his own pet theories, including a common physiological basis for schizophrenia and creativity, and an all-purpose account of disease resulting from a failure to metabolize fatty acids. Although *Medical Hypotheses* was criticized and sometimes ridiculed for its editorial policy, the journal's articles were widely read and highly cited. Indeed, no serious attempt was made to change the journal's explicitly anti-peer review stance even after the Dutch mega-publisher Elsevier acquired the title in 2002.

But all of this changed in 2009, when Horrobin's successor Bruce Charlton accepted an article by Peter Duesberg, the distinguished Berkeley virologist who for the past quarter-century has contested the HIV-basis of AIDS. Duesberg's article argued that the South African government was probably right to follow his advice not to administer anti-retroviral drugs to that country's AIDS sufferers because the HIV-AIDS link remains unproven and the subsequent AIDS-related deaths in that country can be more plausibly explained by other factors. This led scientists associated with the US National Institutes of Health (NIH) to threaten to have all subscriptions to Elsevier titles removed from the National Library of Medicine if the publisher did not withdraw the offending article from publication and henceforth institute peer review at *Medical Hypotheses*, since articles such as Duesberg's have 'potentially negative consequences for public health and the goals of the NIH' (Abdool Karim et al. 2009). Elsevier agreed to all the demands, which eventually meant the sacking of Charlton, who refused to budge as a matter of commitment to Horrobin's editorial principles (Corbyn 2010).

However, lawyers may turn out to be the main beneficiaries of this sorry tale, since Elsevier effectively conceded that publishing only peer-reviewed science constitutes a safeguard to public health. One now waits with incipient *schadenfreude* for a city or state to sue a publisher precisely because its adherence to findings from peer-reviewed science in its journals made for detrimental public health policies. Over a decade ago, I suggested that if universities wished to encourage its faculty to be 'socially relevant' in its pronouncements, then – in the spirit of 'put you money where your mouth is' – they should set aside a fund for paying damages when the advice goes horribly wrong, *especially* when the pronouncements are based on peer-reviewed publications from which no self-respecting university could distance itself (Fuller 2000a: chap. 8).

3 THE EPISTEMIC DIMENSION OF PEER REVIEW: BACKWARD OR FORWARD LOOKING?

Setting aside the motives of research fraudsters and other peer review desperados, a cold 'epistemic' look at the situation reveals that peer reviewers have no choice but to expose themselves to potential fraud. Any article submitted for peer review is an invitation for the peers to assume a risk that effectively lays their collective reputation on the line by validating the author's work as living up to the same standard as the other work they have already validated. To be sure, as disciplinary gatekeepers, the peers understand that they must be always investing in innovative research to signal their field's epistemic growth potential in a crowded market that seeks the same pot of intellectual, political and financial capital. As commercial publishers often see more clearly than the peer reviewers they underwrite, the underlying strategy is 'grow or die'. I shall return to the proactive character of commercial publishers *vis-à-vis* peer review below.

In stressing the moral over the epistemic dimension of the peer review process, I do not wish to imply that peer review as normally practised is completely devoid of epistemic character. However, that character is distinctly *backward looking*. In other words, peer review aims to reward work that has been already done, and for that reason it is important that the work has, indeed, been done. Moreover, peer review's backward-looking character has come to colonize more of the organized knowledge system, as research capacity – the forms of capital required from producing candidate publications for peer review – increasingly depends on prior funding, which is itself increasingly judged on the basis of the track record or pedigree of the researchers involved. Peer review's backward look has been further promoted by the absorption of the academic knowledge system into the larger political economy of intellectual property. To be sure, a journal publication does not carry the same promise of legal enforcement of credit acknowledgement as a patent, but the entitlement to credit in both cases is similar and increasingly salient in the evaluation of the knowledge system, ranging from judgements of individual impact based on citation counts to the rank-ordering of university departments based on the number of high-impact publications.

Lost in all this backwardness is the idea of peer review as a *proactive* process. This problem is especially pronounced nowadays in the case of academic journals. The maturity of an academic field is often signalled by the tendency of the author pool of the field's main journals to constitute a self-organizing market. In that case, journal editors can simply select the best material that passes through the peer review process with minimal prompting on their own part. This *laissez faire* approach is a far cry from the origins of modern publishing, in which today's clearly distinguished roles for 'publisher', 'editor' and 'author' were absent. Until copyright legislation began to separate these roles in the 18th century, the 'author' was the person who stamped his authority on a body of work by commissioning the writers, editing and organizing their works, and then producing and distributing the finished product – typically with considerable content input of his own (Fuller 2002: chap. 2). Such an 'author' was proactive in the manner of an entrepreneur or impresario, in which 'peerage' was effectively conferred on others through extended collaboration, 'participatory peerage', if you will. The last generation of this heroic moment in proactive publishing was epitomized in the career of Benjamin Franklin in colonial America, but its scaled-up fruits also included Ephraim Chambers' London-based *Cyclopaedia*, the prototype for Denis Diderot and Jean D'Alembert's *L'Encyclopédie*, which was in turn emulated – albeit in the politically muted tones characteristic of the Scottish Enlightenment – by the *Encyclopaedia Britannica*.

To be sure, remnants of this old heroic proactive ideal can be found over the last two centuries. A clear case in point is the late 19th/early 20th-century deployment of the academic journal as a discipline-building device attached to a specific university department and a founding editor with a strong intellectual vision. Here one might cite the role of *L'Année Sociologique* under Emile Durkheim at the Sorbonne, *Philosophical Review* founded by Cornell University President Jacob Schurman, and *Isis*, the history of science journal founded at Harvard by George Sarton. A similar strategy was adopted, albeit more fitfully, by the logical positivists in their various vehicles: first, the journals *Erkenntnis* and *Synthese*, while based in Vienna, and then the *International Encyclopedia of Unified Science*, once based in Chicago. In all these cases, editors actively solicited those whom they had identified as fellow-travellers. For example, in their Viennese incarnation, the logical positivists launched a manifesto as a market signal to prospective peers who might be attracted to their idiosyncratically Austro-centric genealogy of 'the scientific version of the world'. But equally important in all these cases, the editors made a point of reviewing a wide range of literature, always in terms of its relevance to the journal's mission. That regular feature alone helped to establish a 'house style of thought' for fields that had yet to accumulate a body of original research.

Many of these originally proactive journal- and book-based movements were eventually incorporated by professional academic bodies, which offered financial security in exchange for their 'bending over backward' (in temporal horizon) by catering to the default tendencies of their clientele. Thus, a decision to run a special issue of a journal on an 'emerging tendency' within a discipline typically requires tricky editorial negotiations. Ironically perhaps, it has been left to the commissioning editors of commercial publishers to seek out nascent intellectual tendencies for the purposes of establishing new journals and book series. In this context, the role of the British publishers Routledge and Sage in setting the global intellectual agenda of cultural and gender studies since the 1980s should not be underestimated. After all, academic publishing houses are historically dependent on the opinions of the resident experts in established departments. In contrast, commercial publishers presume that some sustainable intellectual perspectives have been overlooked, in which case money may be made by encouraging marginalized academics to generate markets for their own distinctive work (Fuller 2002: chap. 3). In this context, the commissioning editor functions as a matchmaker among those sharing common intellectual interests who might go on to seed a peer community by agreeing to join a journal's editorial board. But in the end, because commercial publishing is ultimately run as a business, these prospects are given a short run (e.g. 3–5 years) in which to generate a target level of submissions and subscriptions.

4 PEER REVIEW AS (NOT) SEEN BY SCIENCE JOURNALISTS

So far we have seen that peer review in practice directly enforces moral rather than epistemic norms: misrepresentation of self rather than reality is of paramount concern. Moreover, insofar as peer review does enforce epistemic norms, they tend to be backward not forward looking. Put charitably, peer review aims more to determine whether research has been done well than whether it was worth doing. Indeed, those whose overriding concern is with the value of knowledge *per se* may find problems with peer review's *modus operandi*. In particular, the main source of conflict between the scientific establishment and science journalists is that journalists take more seriously than the scientists themselves that science speaks to the larger philosophical issues concerning human existence, which in turn justifies continued public support of science.

If this claim seems strange, one may think about the conflict as a by-product of scientists' reliance on peer review as a process that not only validates scientific work but also comes to be seen – if only by the scientists themselves – as self-validating. In other words, the very fact that active researchers, often operating from vastly different theoretical orientations, can agree on the value of work for which they are then willing to take collective responsibility through authorized publication is a sign that the work was worth doing. This line of argument was already present in the Charter of the Royal Society of London in 1660, which, in light of England's then-recent history with civil war, implicitly set a standard for dispute resolution that in the future might be emulated by politicians. Indeed, within fifty years, much of the model was adopted by what we now call 'the mother of all parliaments'.

However, this distinguished pedigree typically fails to sway science journalists, who are less impressed by the normative standard that peer review sets for reaching ideological consensus than the more prosaic tendency of scientists to fail to live up to those avowed standards. In fact, journalists see scientists living up to another set of standards that are only misleadingly captured by the phrase, 'peer review' but may be less misleadingly called 'mutual protection racket' (Fuller 1997: chap. 4). Three features of peer review in practice come to mind:

1 Reviewer and reviewed are very often not 'peers' in the strict sense. On the whole, reviewers represent a more elite sector of the research community than the authors whose work they review. Not surprisingly, articles accepted for publication tend to have more elite authors than those rejected. Worst of all, the ideas in rejected articles often end up appearing in print a few years later under the name of a more elite author: coincidence or conspiracy? Either way, little wonder that non-elite researchers with controversial views have preferred to take their chances by going directly to the mass media with their findings. Moreover, there is little incentive (other than 'good scientific citizenship') to participate in peer review, since the process is both anonymous and time-consuming, which means unpaid labour. Although journal publishers periodically flirt with providing financial incentives for peer reviewers, these are of limited value because the peers themselves are the main beneficiaries: i.e. however costly the process is for peers, it is mainly in their own – and no one else's – interest to review the work of other researchers.

2 Peer review's validation procedure rarely involves a direct test of the knowledge claims for which the author wishes to receive credit. It is nothing like Ralph Nader's *Consumer Reports* or the US Food and Drug Administration's health and safety tests. Instead, submitted articles are judged on what psychologists call their 'face validity', to wit: is it reasonable

to suppose that a competent researcher operating within the stated theoretical framework and the specified methodological parameters would acquire data of the sort indicated and interpret them in the terms suggested by the author? Here the peer reviewer is looking to internal consistency as a sign of external validity. While such a heuristic is powerless in the face of a perfect forgery, it does provide a means of capturing such common forms of research malpractice as massaged data, sample overgeneralization, and theory misinterpretation. In the early days of the Royal Society, when those likely to submit articles to its *Proceedings* knew each other as 'Fellows', much was made of the 'trustworthiness' of the scientific reports, which alluded to the character of the reporters. However, as peer review extended its epistemic authority to all researchers in a given field, the clubby character of trustworthiness yielded to a more anonymized, forensic assessment of submitted pieces that privileges being 'correct on the page', which is to leave as little as possible to the imagination. To a science journalist, this approach still does not get much beyond biblical criticism, since the peer reviewer never actually directly encounters the empirical basis for the knowledge claims.

3 Peer review involves what economists call 'transaction costs' that are borne by the reviewers, unless they can be offloaded to the authors. After all, if the peer reviewers are about to take collective responsibility for an author's research, they have an interest in publishing the version with which they are most comfortable. However, instead of the reviewers themselves writing additional pieces that correct or contest in detail what an author has written, the reviewers can make publication conditional on the author's incorporation of such criticism in a revised version. Thus, the potential for displaying intellectual conflict is pre-empted – some would say 'sublimated' – through a negotiated settlement. At one level, this is a win-win situation. The author gets published, while the peers continue to give the impression that the field's knowledge base is subject to steady, cumulative growth. However, in this backroom deal, the journalist sees proof of what economists call 'rent-seeking' behaviour: a situation that would otherwise allow for genuine epistemic growth by forcing both sides to defend and possibly alter their positions is replaced by one in which the author agrees to depend on the peers for validation. The author's individuality is essentially bought. Thus, a common condition for publication is that the author must add references to other putatively related work that the author may not have read – let alone been influenced by – but serves to reinforce the peers' sense

> of the lines of epistemic descent. The author effectively yields some of her originality to acquire legitimation from retrofitted precursors and fellow-travellers whom the peers regard as 'politically correct' authorities. When these retrofitted sources have themselves published in the journal in which the author seeks publication, the author's acquiescence helps to boost what scientometricians call the journal's 'impact factor', which measures the likelihood that others will cite articles published in a given journal, which in turn perpetuates the appearance of the journal's centrality to its field.

In short, science journalists see peer review as a theory of scientific governance that has yet to find an adequate practice. Under the circumstances, it should come as no surprise that science journalists have given significant publicity to scientific opinions that have circumvented, if not been outright condemned, by the scientific peer review process. Examples abound, including HIV-AIDS denialism, cold fusion, creationism, and climate change scepticism. As we have seen, there is perhaps good reason to distrust that peer review is capable of giving a fair hearing to exceptionally challenging views. Indeed, rather than presuming that opposing sides of a scientific issue deserve equal time, journalists typically see themselves as redressing the scientific establishment's misrepresentation of the side it has come to condemn with such apparent unanimity. To be sure, scientists are prone to condemn such journalistic attempts at 'even-handedness' as ignorant arrogance.

A more illuminating assessment of the situation would start by noting that both scientists and journalists are committed to knowledge as a 'universally available public good'. However, they interpret key terms in that phrase rather differently. The main source of this difference is that journalists believe that the sort of intelligence that separates their readers from scientists is a matter of degree, not kind. In effect, journalists espouse a vulgar logical positivism in their insistence that anything worth saying is reducible to something that anyone could judge for herself by using her senses and ordinary powers of reasoning. In that respect, 'everyman' is potentially a scientific peer capable of judging cutting-edge research for herself. All that matters is perspicuous presentation – the main task for journalists. In stark contrast, scientists are inclined to believe that specialist training imparts a certain cast of mind that is qualitatively different from the sorts of judgements that even well-informed amateurs might make. It follows that science journalists would better spend their time informing the public about whose judgement they should and should not trust, based on what has and has not successfully passed the peer review process. This 'underlabouring' version of science journalism is very much alive and well in, say, Ben Goldacre, the award-winning, Oxford-trained medical scientist who writes the weekly 'Bad Science' column for the (London) *Guardian*.

5 PEER REVIEW FROM THE INSIDE: CAN ONE REMAIN UNCYNICAL?

Peer review may have many invidious features, but the one on which science journalists cast the harshest light is its capacity to generate closure on the creditworthiness of a given piece of research. Such 'inter-rater reliability', as psychologists call it, may be explained in several ways. If we take an uncynical view, the predominance of peer consensus simply reflects that a field possesses objective standards of assessment – that there exists a domain about which one may make demonstrably true or false claims. Indeed, the fact that interdisciplinary peer review panels at very competitive research funding agencies generally reach agreement without too much trouble suggests that academia's higher echelon is populated by those who defer to distinguished colleagues outside their sphere of expertise, while presuming that their own expertise will be respected at the appropriate time. That such mutual expectations are borne out in practice was the conclusion drawn by the most intensive participant-observation study of the peer review process at US public and private sector funders in the humanities and the social sciences, Lamont (2009).

But even this work can provide ammunition for cynics. It turns out that it is harder to secure the best grants than to get published in the best journals: 'Grants and fellowships are becoming important as academic signals of excellence, especially because the proliferation of journals has made the number of publications of academics a less reliable measure of their status' (Lamont 2009: 15). Scarcity of funds is less negotiable than scarcity of journal pages. Indeed, there is a long history of academics who, faced with poor acceptance rates of their work in the established disciplinary journals, have gone on to found journals devoted to their specialities, which in turn have acquired established reputations. Notwithstanding the intellectual trail-blazing qualities of such journals, from Lamont's standpoint this practice amounts to currency inflation in the academic credit market. Indeed, today's proliferation of academic journals on the internet appears to be modelled on the fiscal policy of the Weimar Republic.

Against this backdrop, the mutual expectations of peer deference produces what Lamont calls 'conspicuous collegiality', the courtly discourse that appears in the face-to-face peer review panels at the funding agencies. Thus, the conspicuously collegial panellists ostentatiously defend the standards of their own discipline while deferring graciously to the standards of other disciplinary practitioners.

They are mindful of disciplinary boundaries to such an extent that, in their final evaluations, they readily sacrifice more reckless, typically younger colleagues whose grant proposals threaten to 'transgress' the epistemic *cordon sanitaire* defined by those boundaries. Here, Lamont's reliance of Karin Knorr-Cetina's (1999) conception of disciplines as 'epistemic cultures' serves to reinforce – if not simply repeat in more abstract terms – the panellists' own tendencies to stereotype their fields for purposes of boundary maintenance. While Lamont herself invokes Charles Tilly's concept 'opportunity hoarding', that is simply another way of talking about what we have observed as the 'rent-seeking' tendency of academic disciplines, whereby disciplines perpetuate epistemic hierarchies by monopolizing access to the enabling conditions for key activities (Lamont 2009: 37). All along, both Lamont and her informants presume that a good interdisciplinary project must demonstrate mastery of the constitutive disciplines, a quality that panellists appear to think they can identify with relative ease, though (Lamont admits) such projects are never discussed in sufficient detail to allow readers to reach an independent judgement on the matter.

One classic social theoretic concept that makes a fleeting appearance in Lamont (2009) is *corruption*, the identification of the public good with an exclusionary sense of self-interest, which is more accurately rendered by the concept of 'club goods' (discussed in the next section). Put more metaphysically, the corrupt person does not allow the concerns of the spirit to transcend those of the body. For example, the trademark indignation about French academic life registered by Lamont's erstwhile mentor, Pierre Bourdieu (1990), was a response to the corruption he perceived among his colleagues, who collectively reproduced their society's class structure in their intellectual discriminations, or 'judgements of taste'. Bourdieu understood this phenomenon more as a function than a cause of the existing class structure. Thus, he did not anticipate the sort of corruption that Lamont's account unwittingly suggests, namely, that when it comes to allocating research funds, academic peer review panels are sites for the outright manufacture of an academic class system that might otherwise not exist, or at least not so markedly.

Here, it is worth recalling that the 'peerage' implied in the phrase 'peer review' is traditionally to do with the equality of inquirers in both giving and receiving criticism. In other words, the peers are presumed to be not only equally competent for purposes of passing judgement, but also equally resilient in the face of negative judgement. This principle made sense in the early days of the Royal Society, when members were for the most part of independent means, and scientific research required a greater dedication of time than money. However, once research became undoable without external funding, and peer review was used as the principle of allocation, judgements started to be passed not simply over one's research results but over one's very capacity to do research.

Corruption is a very likely – if perhaps unintended – consequence of this arrangement, since the peers are being forced to treat grant-seekers as capital investments. It becomes virtually impossible to judge proposals without considering the opportunity costs, track record and prospects of an academic field in which the judge herself is a player. Implicit realization of this fact explains why 'affirmative action' and 'diversity management' considerations matter when academic peers are allocating research funds but not journal pages. However, Lamont leaves the impression that the conspicuous collegiality of academic peer review is not an elaborate exercise in corruption simply because those who engage in it invest enormous time and effort, which she takes to be an indirect measure of sincerity. In contrast, I am left with a renewed sense of the value of Bourdieu's demystified approach to the academic field.

But peer review's tendency to assign too much epistemic weight to what is, in effect, a glorified version of groupthink is perhaps not nearly as sinister as a by-product of that tendency – namely, the reification of academic judgement. Thus, even though a given set of peer reviewers may only somewhat overlap in their reasons for accepting or rejecting an article for publication, the common bottom-line judgement is what matters, which in turn may be converted into a quantity that figures in the various knowledge-based metrics used in research evaluation, what Nicholas Rescher (2007) has called 'epistemetrics'. Moreover, this point applies to not only which articles get published but also which ones get cited. If the former indicators capture whether research has been done well, the latter indicators increasingly serve as a proxy for whether research was worth doing – a *de facto* 'invisible hand' of post-publication peer review tracking epistemic merit in the marketplace of academic ideas (Mirowski 2004). However, the main problems with peer review's easy reification go beyond the simple misrepresentation of academic judgement. More important is the distortion of academic motivation that it encourages. Here, two issues stand out: (1) the bias towards consensus while the dynamics of inquiry favours disagreement; (2) the incentive that reification offers to 'gaming the system' by engaging in the sorts of practices that were associated above with the 'mutual protection racket' aspect of peer review.

6 SHALL IT BE 'OPEN ACCESS' OR 'OPEN SCIENCE'?

I would hate to leave the impression that peer review – outside the proactive mode promoted by publishers – is a remedy worse than the ailment it is meant to address. On the contrary, it has a clear but circumscribed role in the governance of the knowledge system. In particular, peer review is a good mechanism for focusing and channelling disagreement – which is to say, providing auxiliary constraints on the flow of academic discourse. This role was immediately recognized in the first modern scientific societies and was typically performed by the society's secretary (e.g. Henry Oldenburg in England and Marin Mersenne in France). Before the establishment of academic journals, new research was sent in the form of correspondence to the secretary who then distributed it to society members.

The secretary took care to correct obvious errors of fact, remove infelicities of expression that could lead to both personal and scientific misunderstanding among the members, query or curb overstretched inferences, and censor outright irreligious or politically inflammatory statements. However, the secretary did not attempt to adjudicate on the proposed knowledge claims or even compel the author to bear a specific burden of proof. In this way, the secretary remained a peer of the author by avoiding the temptation to become a second-order critic – or, worse, inquisitor. In terms of today's standards, it resulted in a wider range of intellectual starting points and endpoints being seriously entertained. Indeed, reinstating the secretarial role of peer review (even though it could no longer be a single individual) would allow today's scientific controversies to be played out in a more epistemically edifying fashion.

As things stand today, all too often peer review is used to exclude radically alternative intellectual starting points. This in turn forces the mavericks to non-peer reviewed forums that are often ill-equipped to catch technical errors. These errors – the sort of thing that a secretarial peer would have caught – may not affect the substance of the maverick knowledge claims, but they do provide a further pretext – incompetence – for the establishment's refusal to give a proper hearing to the mavericks. Thus, it is only the authoritarian appeal to peer review, so alien to the early modern scientific societies, that needs to be ended – and preferably replaced by something truer to its original spirit, namely, a more modest office focused on error-correction.

At the same time, journalists and other peer review cynics have a point. The relatively similar training and career orientation of peers create common expectations about the qualities that should be possessed by publishable – and, increasingly, fundable – work. This creates a sense of solidarity that is evident even in the so-called *open access* movement, which would have academics take their business away from commercial publishers who charge increasingly high fees for academics to get access to their own work. Interestingly, the world's wealthiest university, Harvard, has spearheaded this movement by exhorting its academics to migrate to self-organizing open access journals – operating on the assumption that commercial publishers are irrelevant to the maintenance of the quality control standards associated with peer review (Rosen 2012). But as we have seen, publishers are more than the parasitic rent-seekers that this image presumes. Minimally they impose a discipline that might be otherwise lacking in academics (i.e. the regular delivery of research results), but historically they have lured academics from their disciplinary comfort zones by providing opportunities to reconfigure their fields.

From this standpoint, the open access movement should be seen as nothing more – but also nothing less – than a consumer revolt, academic style. No one in this revolt is calling for what is sometimes called 'extended peer review' (whereby relevant non-academic stakeholders operate as knowledge gatekeepers), let alone the abandonment of science's normal technicality. Indeed, much of the moral suasion of the open access movement would be dissipated if it complained not only about the price of academic journals but also the elite character of the peer review process itself. After all, only the presumption of self-recognition among the 'peers' in the peer review process gives the appearance that publishers play a 'merely administrative' function. As of this writing, this pose of mutual recognition is easier to maintain in the natural than the social sciences because of its greater agreement on what counts as a 'soluble problem' and how one goes about solving it – that is, what Kuhn (1970) recognized as these disciplines' 'normal science' functions.

Put another way, the open access movement fails to appreciate the prospecting work done by publishers that cuts against the default self-reproducing tendencies of the peer review process, when left entirely in the hands of academics. In effect, open access is limited to making research cheaper to access by those who already possess the skills to do so but are held back by such 'artificial' barriers as publishers' paywalls. Nothing in the movement bears on questions concerning how one might democratize knowledge production itself – such as how research credit might be distributed across students, informants, etc.; how one might select research topics that people find worthwhile; how accessibility to a wide variety, including non-specialist, audiences might be made a desideratum for securing publication (Bell 2012).

In short, *open access* relates to what genuine democratizers of inquiry call *open science* as *club goods* relate to *public goods* in economics (cf. Marginson 2007). Open access is designed to ensure the smooth flow of club goods – namely, that those who have already paid into the system – that is, by virtue of having invested in acquiring the relevant social and intellectual capital – are its primary, if not exclusive, beneficiaries. This sense of 'paying into the system' runs deeper than the usual – and more misleading – open access claim that state-funded research, even if commercially published, should be made freely available to taxpayers. After all, public access to academic publications in their normal form is a mere pseudo-benefit, given that most people would not know what to make of them.

Whereas public goods are governed by the idea that it would cost more to exclude people who do not pay into the system than simply to include them, club goods operate on the principle that the goods themselves would lose value if the terms of membership were not strictly observed. Thus, defenders of science as a public good worry about the foregone benefits that might result from the overzealous pursuit of potentially productive 'free riders', while those who defend science as a club good are more concerned that fully paid-up members get their money's worth, namely, an entitlement to exercise a certain epistemic advantage over those very 'free riders'. In this respect, by presuming the club good model, open access campaigners take knowledge to be a kind of *positional good*, whereby a good's scarcity is definitive of its value (cf. Fuller 2005). However, there is a twist. Whereas theorists of positional goods are normally concerned with the depreciation of value that comes from too many people having access to a good, in the open access case the source of depreciation is too *limited* access – namely, that those already capable of using the knowledge find it too expensive to access it.

Clearly, when taken as descriptors of knowledge systems, 'open' and 'public' stand in an interesting tension with each other. They are by no means contradictory but they may be orthogonal, such that a 2x2 matrix of possibilities would include not only 'open and public' (i.e. knowledge as Enlightenment) and 'closed and private' (i.e. knowledge as intellectual property) but also two other quadrants: 'open and private' and 'closed and public'. The former corresponds to a classical free market for knowledge, the latter to a Soviet-style planned knowledge economy. These two possibilities – perhaps especially the former – are obscured by a tendency to confuse unboundedness with universality: openness addresses the first concept, publicity the second. In other words, to say that knowledge is allowed to migrate freely is not necessarily to say that it will reach everyone who might have use for it. On this basis the social democratic welfare state could lay claim to being the sole providers of knowledge as a public good. It is a mark of our neo-liberal political economy of knowledge production that *openness* and *publicity* are so easily confused.

Symptomatic of this confusion is a tendency to ignore the spontaneously path-dependent nature of knowledge production. In philosophical terms, the *context of justification* is much more embedded in the *context of discovery* than one might like to admit. (The reverse is also the case, which helps to explain the limits on the discoveries that can be made at a given time, leading potential innovators to narrow their vision to second-guessing what the relevant market will take.) Indeed, the normative force of the logical positivist and Popperian injunction to divorce the two contexts is itself a measure of their default historical linkage. Under normal circumstances, it is presumed that the person who originates a knowledge claim can capitalize on that initial advantage, perhaps resulting in a monopoly. Academic life is in this respect more invidious than business because, instead of having the law safeguard original advantage through copyrights and patents, which entrepreneurs are then motivated to overturn or circumvent, academics themselves have a vested interest in establishing the advantage of their predecessors as an indirect means of promoting themselves. In the end, one sees a putatively 'open' system resulting in a scheme that resembles a Mafia.

7 CONCLUSIONS: LESSONS FOR THE ACADEMIC CAESAR

In light of the above considerations, an interesting version of the time-honoured constitutional strategy of 'checks and balances' may be adopted by the Academic Caesar. It involves playing the natural openness of entrepreneurial publishers against the natural public-mindedness of Humboldtian scholar-teachers – resulting in some satisfying institutional synthesis, a 'University 2.0', so to speak. As I already suggested in the previous chapter when discussing academic rentiership, both entrepreneurs and Humboldtians are engaged in 'creative destruction', but of somewhat different knowledge markets. Applied to the present case, on the one hand, publishers are keen to displace the hegemony of disciplinary structures by locating uncharted intellectual terrain and reconfiguring academic networks. On the other, academics keen to translate their research into classroom practice dissipate the epistemic advantage, if not monopoly, that the original researchers – possibly including oneself – have enjoyed. Indeed, that elimination of an original advantage may be organized so as to provide an incentive for academics to engage the services of publishers to move into relatively fallow fields of inquiry.

Thus, the Academic Caesar would enable publishers and academics to engage symbiotically in their complementary movements of creative destruction. In its most concrete and controversial form, this policy could bring publishers into the governing structure and staffing of the university, thereby ensuring that the university acquires more of the proactive orientation of a proper corporate enterprise. But why might this prospect be attractive to commercial publishers? I end with a 'modest proposal' to transfer peer review entirely to the publishers, perhaps as part of a larger merger agreement. To be sure, such a move goes against the grain of the 'open access' movement, yet it highlights the deep structural problems in the relationship between the production and evaluation of knowledge in today's neo-liberal world.

Suppose you're an executive at a transnational academic publishing firm struggling with the problem of getting academics to referee articles for publication. Your starting assumption so far has been that academics should be willing to do this for free because they realize that their credibility relies on 'peer review'. So your policy has been not to pay them anything – or at least not anything substantial (e.g. the 30-day free access to journals that their universities already supply for free). But the strategy does not seem to work. Academics either refuse to referee outright or they accept the task but then turn in the report well beyond the deadline, as if they know that you have no choice but to wait. Moreover, they are right. Meanwhile, as we have seen, academics are increasingly taking refuge in 'open source' internet-based platforms that appear to operate with minimal overhead yet profess some measure of peer review. The net result is a haemorrhaging of your core client base. What to do?

The solution is simply to treat peer reviewing as an in-house publishing function, on the model of the R&D division of the modern corporation. The only reason why no one has proposed this is that the 'lean and mean' postmodern corporation sheds its R&D division and outsources innovation to universities who, faced with their own crisis of legitimation, gladly do capital's bidding in a way that saves firms money while making themselves look 'relevant'. And while this strategy of managing the *production* of knowledge may well prove a 'win-win' strategy for the corporate and academic worlds in our neo-liberal world, it cannot be generalized to the *evaluation* of knowledge. Neo-liberalism, after all, depends on clear market signals, not least in the knowledge market. Not only must these signals be reliable, but they must also match the pulse of the market. From this standpoint, academic evaluation proceeds much too slowly for the quite simple reason that academics are valued mainly for being productive and not evaluative.

You cannot usually get a professorship simply on the basis of vast connoisseurship of the scientific literature, which enables you to spot frauds, fallacies, prospects and brilliance at a glance. People who spend more time reading than writing tend not to meet the threshold of chair-worthiness. Nevertheless, it is precisely such people who uphold the distinctiveness of the 'academic' brand of knowledge production. In that case, it may be the job of publishers to rescue the academic brand – from academia itself – by hiring these people on a part- or full-time basis. In strict economic terms, to ensure quality control in academic knowledge production, peer review may need to be internalized as a regular publishing cost.

It would be hard to see how universities could object to this policy, as they themselves offer little, if any, incentive for academics to become involved in the evaluation of their peers' work. From a neo-liberal perspective, it simply marks a segmentation of the knowledge market: on the one hand, universities appear ill-equipped to support activities surrounding research evaluation; on the other, academic publishers have an interest in promoting the value of academic research. This would seem, then, to be a match made in heaven.

If this scenario comes to pass – which is entirely possible – it will be because academia has so far failed to play its hand well in the neo-liberal game. Neo-liberal policymakers already know that much truly innovative knowledge is not – and never has been – produced in universities. In this respect, they are instinctively 'postmodern' (Lyotard 1983). Nevertheless, they have usually expected universities to provide the testing ground or selection mechanism for these various ideas and schemes, to see which merit more widespread distribution. But if universities fail to step up to the plate, perhaps because they overestimate the value of sheer knowledge production, then it is only reasonable that publishers – whose own viability is directly affected by problems in academic quality control – take matters into their own hands and encourage universities to outsource their evaluative functions to them. In any case, a market should be created for knowledge connoisseurs, and in today's world publishers are better placed than 'research-intensive' universities to do so.

3

MACROECONOMIC KNOWLEDGE POLICY FOR ACADEMIC CAESARS AND THEIR WOULD-BE REGULATORS

1 KNOWLEDGE IN SEARCH OF A LEVEL OF ECONOMIC ANALYSIS IT CAN CALL ITS OWN

This chapter argues that the pursuit of knowledge as an end in itself – that is, 'scientific inquiry' in its strict sense – can be justified only from within a macroeconomic framework that fosters the production of public goods. The argument follows closely the need for either a *welfare state* or *market socialism* to ensure the steady generation of public goods. Even we presume (controversially) that individuals know their own interests and capacities best, it does not follow that they know the interests and capacities of others sufficiently well to be confident that between them the right sort of knowledge will be generated to enable all of them to achieve their ends. It is therefore more rational for people to redistribute their effort – and income – towards collective epistemic projects before pursuing more personalized goals. Put another way, because we generally do not know what knowledge will do the most good for us, it is best to set about producing all knowledge possible. However, and crucially, it also follows that we should also set about to make the most of that knowledge. Economists tend to assume that the problem of public goods is solved once their production has been secured. However, there remains the problem of the optimal utilization of the goods so produced. Thus, in what follows we shall return to the phenomenon of *undiscovered public knowledge* introduced in the previous chapter.

The university has been historically the most important site for such collective projects to manufacture knowledge as a public good. To be sure, the university has required its own internal redistributive schemes to counteract the effects of what the sociologist Robert Merton (1977) called 'cumulative advantage', namely, the inertial transmission of privilege – often reflecting more societally pervasive forms of privilege – through the knowledge system itself. Overall this invites a more general challenge, again from a macroeconomic perspective, of the pre-eminence of the university as a stand-alone institution in knowledge policy. We shall consider the various dimensions of this challenge, mindful of the extended spatial and temporal horizons needed for public goods to demonstrate their full value. It concludes with an examination of an exemplary attempt to administer the universities as part of an integrated national education policy. The Althoff System, named for the responsible minister, succeeded in making Germany the premier scientific nation by the start of the First World War. Yet, such success must be set against the ease with which a similar policy later enabled German academia to be co-opted in the Nazi period.

It is difficult to justify scientific inquiry except from a macroeconomic perspective. By 'scientific inquiry' I mean the production of knowledge as a public good, the sort of thing that is paradigmatically produced in universities, understood as a unique organizational form. This activity cannot be easily justified in *micro*economic terms because the locus of value in science lies mainly offstage from the particular transactions on display in the agora between producers and consumers of knowledge (Fuller 2003). On the one hand, as Newton famously declared, the putative knowledge producer is always 'standing on the shoulders of giants' (and many of lesser stature who stand *behind* them) and is distinctive merely in seeing more by a sufficient margin to attract the interest of the current round of knowledge consumers. On the other hand, the putative knowledge consumer, understood as a taxpayer, research client or fee-paying student, is likely to have whatever advantage she accrues from the transaction quickly undercut by the many others who later come to enjoy a similar benefit at an even lower cost.

In short, science is a conundrum for the strict microeconomic theorist because the people who officially offer themselves as traders in the knowledge market are arguably neither the ones most responsible for the product nor the ones likely to benefit the most from it (Fuller 2003). Thus, the author of a new piece of research in a scientific journal is building on the work of authors and offering it openly for others to use. Of course, science can be reformatted to the liking of microeconomists, via intellectual property legislation, which makes it harder both for later knowledge producers to build on their predecessors and for knowledge consumers to free-ride on so-called early adopters. The increasing centrality of citation metrics in the evaluation of individual scientific performance, as well as the greater attention generally given to the proper assignment of credit in academic work, are already major steps in that direction. Sometimes this tendency, associated with a postmodern, post-industrial and post-academic approach to knowledge policy, is touted as 'finally' bringing science into line with economic realities. However, this development is better counted as just another instance of the narrowing of economic horizons following the eclipse of Marx and Keynes by Smith and Hayek. It rides on the back of a now quarter-century campaign to reduce the macro- to microeconomic. There have always been strong macroeconomic grounds for the generous finance of scientific inquiry. The problem is that people today do not believe in macroeconomics the way they once did, and unsurprisingly they act in accordance with their disbelief.

Belief in the existence of a macro-level entity, the 'economy', that exhibits a logic above and beyond the aggregation of market transactions has waxed and waned in the history of economics. Even Adam Smith may be read as either a micro- or a macroeconomic theorist. Does the talismanic phrase 'invisible hand' imply that there is no hand guiding the economy or that the hand is so subtle that only policy adepts can perceive it through the mass of exchanges? Both readings informed the Austrian school of economics that reinvented liberalism's defining tensions in the context of a cosmopolitan Catholic culture, a century after it had first appeared in the cosmopolitan Protestant culture of Britain (Hacohen 2000: chap. 10). The reading of the invisible hand that stressed its invisibility produced the 'Right Smithians', Ludwig Mises and Friedrich Hayek, while the reading that stressed its handedness produced the 'Left Smithians', Joseph Schumpeter and Karl Polanyi (Fuller 2006a).

Right and Left Smithians may be distinguished by their answers to two questions: (1) Is there such a thing as 'market failure'? Left Smithians base their robust faith in the corrective powers of the state on the alleged frequency of such failures, whereas Right Smithians maintain that those who think they see market failure have themselves failed to correctly define the market in question. (2) Do statistics and their algebraic manipulation (aka econometrics) have a role to play in economic policymaking? Left Smithians stake their epistemic authority on the prospects for such quantification, whereas Right Smithians are closet phenomenologists who treat numbers as a poor replacement for lived experience (aka tacit knowledge). From a strict historical standpoint, the Left Smithians were closer to Smith's original sense of 'political economy'. Smith's speculations about the beliefs and desires of individual traders were offered not as irreducible foundations of economic life, but as levers that policymakers might manipulate to increase the overall wealth of society.

However, Left Smithians differ from pure Communists in seeing the value of markets and states as trading off against each other: the failure of one may be compensated by the strength of the other. This may be understood in terms of two macroeconomic strategies that became clearly distinguished after the Second World War: the *welfare state* and *market socialism*. The former portrays the state as acting through the central bank and the tax system to referee the play of market forces to ensure that the economy remains in equilibrium. The naturalness of markets is assumed, but mainly as an expression of human egoism. This necessitates the watchful eye of the state, which redistributes the surplus of the rich to the poor, thereby inhibiting the concentration of wealth in society. In contrast, the market socialist extends her watchful eye to the very formation of markets. They are not the natural expression of human egoism, but merely what B.F. Skinner called 'operants', namely, something people spontaneously do, perhaps out of instinct but with no clear end in sight. Markets are thus manipulable, ideally by a central planning board that sets up socially desirable economic targets and then invites market competition for their achievement.

The difference in emphasis between the welfare state and market socialism is striking. The former sees the state as tinkering on the margins of market-driven processes, while the latter empowers the state to set the parameters within which markets may legitimately function. Nevertheless, for both, the macroeconomic impulse was originally tied to the use of markets as a relatively unobtrusive mechanism for improving behaviour, or, put generously, enabling the development of moral character: people are sufficiently rational that, given adequate incentives, they will voluntarily alter their behaviour in accordance with the policymaker's plan (Fuller 2006a). Specifically, something previously deemed opposed to one's interests, whether it be to pay more taxes or to compete in markets where one lacks a natural advantage, may come to be seen as crucial to satisfying those very interests.

Thus, a macroeconomic policymaker aims to convert *prima facie* obstacles into design features in the environment by persuading everyone that each of their goals is more likely to be achieved by less direct means that all of them can pursue simultaneously than by each pursuing divergent means they regard as most efficient. This rhetorical artifice is as good a definition of 'norm' (i.e. *nomos*, legislation, as opposed to *physis*, nature's law) as one is ever likely to get (cf. Simon 1977). Moreover, such a conception has the knock-on effect of forcing everyone to recognize each other as implicated in a common fate, which in turn serves to inculcate social solidarity (Fuller and Collier 2004: chap. 7). To be sure, this chain of reasoning has always had an air of alchemy because of its purported conversion of a physical liability into an intellectual virtue. Here Left and Right Smithians may be distinguished by their willingness to count under the *beneficent* rubric of 'unintended consequences' indirectly caused changes of mind, not merely unanticipated material windfalls. Left Smithians have been clearly willing, which has significant implications in the realm of knowledge policy. It opens the door to an idea friendly to the interests of the university – namely, that an agency that requires everyone to spend some time pursuing knowledge for its own sake may be the most efficient means to enable large numbers of disparately interested people to achieve their respective ends in the same society.

In short, macroeconomics provides an interesting twist on Marx's Eleventh Thesis on Feuerbach: 'Philosophers have so far only interpreted the world; the point is to change it'. For, if the world is changed in just the right way, people will interpret it so that their own interests are served by trying to benefit everyone. An important benchmark for this perspective was John Stuart Mill's early appeal to what we now call the principle of diminishing marginal utility to justify redistributive tax schemes: the rich benefit so little from each additional increment of income that the harm caused by its transfer to a much poorer person would be offset by the benefit the poor person might then enjoy. For Mill, a reasonable cost of maintaining a free market in labour and capital, goods and services, is that no one should enjoy so great a market advantage as to impede the ability of others to trade effectively. From that standpoint, diminishing marginal utility is a normative principle based on a 'free market' that does not happen 'freely' (i.e. spontaneously) but requires its active maintenance. Bismarck established the first welfare state in this spirit by blackmailing the German rich to fund the health and education of the poor, lest the latter refuse to defend the nation in times of war or, worse, decide to stage a revolution themselves.

However, even in his own day, Mill's argument for redistribution was challenged by the UK's first professor of economics, William Stanley Jevons, who observed that raising the efficiency of coal use in manufacturing raised coal use overall. Jevons inferred more generally that increased productivity is not self-economizing but results in still more production (Fuller 2006b: chap. 3). In short, the rich can always find ways to use any normatively defined 'surplus' to generate still more wealth that (presumably) improves, in a 'trickle-down' fashion, general welfare – all without formal redistribution. While Jevons' argument struck both Mill and Marx as tailor-made to enable the rich to increase their dominance over the poor, when transferred to the arena of knowledge policy, it becomes recognizable as what Robert Merton (1977) called the 'principle of cumulative advantage' (or the 'Matthew Effect'), which justifies the entitlement of those high in knowledge-based cultural capital to accumulate still more students, grants, publications and citations. The assumption here is that the maturation of science – understood in the spirit of a Kuhnian paradigm – is accompanied by an increase in the entry costs for new contributors, who need to acquire more specialized knowledge, typically from a restricted range of locations. The advances of knowledge made possible by this narrowing of the scientific horizons supposedly outweigh the surface justice championed by countervailing affirmative action policies. However, Fuller (2003) has expressed doubts about the wisdom of the Merton–Kuhn trade-off.

Finally, over a century after it was first proposed, Mill's redistributivist argument was hit by a still subtler psychic quandary. Even granting that each additional increment of wealth matters less to the rich than to the poor, nevertheless the rich are hurt more by having that increment removed than had they never possessed it in the first place (Kahneman and Tversky 1984). For those interested in making good on Mill's vision, this would appear to justify a progressive consumption – not income – tax that charges people according to how much they can pay to acquire comparable benefits. Thus, contrary to the trend in capitalist countries, as people become richer, they would pay the same, not a smaller, percentage of their income for the same goods and services. A version familiar from the higher education sector is the difference in tuition fees charged in the US, where private universities officially charge the highest fees in the world but, in practice, the fees are heavily discounted according to ability to pay. Thus, the poor can benefit without the rich feeling they have been overcharged.

To be sure, progressive consumption taxes are most persuasive when the goods and services are those to which everyone, regardless of financial status, is entitled to have. (In that case, why are food and shelter not subject to progressive consumption taxes? And might not another psychic quandary arise from a poor person forced to choose between an educational 'handout' and no special treatment at all.) On the research front, to prevent the principle of cumulative advantage from becoming an inertial principle of knowledge policy, funders might require successful scientists to improve on previous levels of knowledge production in order to maintain current levels of funding. (Of course, a Machiavellian policymaker could then pit the entire knowledge sector as a whole against other sectors, as in the UK, where overall increases in efficiency have merely served to hold the line in the face of threatened funding cuts.)

2 WHEN THE MACRO-LEVEL IS THOUGHT TO 'EMERGE' FROM MICRO-LEVEL TRANSACTIONS: THE PROBLEM OF UNDISCOVERED PUBLIC KNOWLEDGE

No defence of a macroeconomic perspective on knowledge policy would be complete without observing how it differs from microeconomic justifications associated with the minimization of 'transaction costs', say, in the work of Ronald Coase and Douglass North. According to this view, the state and other institutions emerge as an unintended consequence of the need to maintain the level of trust necessary for the smooth exchange of goods and services between strangers in the marketplace (Seabright 2004). From this perspective, academic credentials and peer-reviewed journals function as 'market signals' that enable prospective employers and clients, both academic and non-academic, to anticipate reliably the knowledge-based properties of the people and products on offer without having to go through the potentially expensive process of checking for oneself (Fuller 1996). Indeed, universities may appear exceptionally efficient because they seem to perform this function spontaneously without any additional charge to the employers and clients who benefit most directly. Then again, efficiency is a virtue that free-riders are especially well positioned to detect in others.

However, the transaction cost approach suffers from two related problems when regarded as a normative basis for knowledge policy: (1) It assumes that, left to their own devices, traders would actually develop a sufficiently explicit and long-term interest in knowledge to dedicate the relevant resources to quality control, say, through dedicating part of their profits to the maintenance of universities. (2) It assumes that the emergent standards of quality control would be applied with sufficient consistency to mimic behaviour normally associated with an interest in knowledge 'for its own sake'. Taken together, these two problems suggest that the transaction cost approach is really interested in knowledge on a 'need-to-know' basis, perhaps because it is difficult to imagine who in the marketplace would come to regard the sheer production of high-quality knowledge as an esteem indicator or identity marker rather than simply a by-product of whatever other qualities on which the knowledge producer would base her esteem or identity.

If economic rationality consists of doing the most with the least in the service of one's ends, then economically rational agents will be keen to cut corners whenever the odds of success are reasonably good. (And, of course, if *everyone* thinks this way, then even if you get caught, that is not likely to be so bad, since it is merely a matter of luck that you, not one of your competitors, suffered that fate.)

Unsurprisingly, then, the logic of transaction costs encourages a cynical account of knowledge-based institutions like disciplines and universities: the academics who dedicate themselves to the existence of such institutions manifest the resourcefulness of people who have failed as first-order market traders. Taking a page from Nietzsche's *The Genealogy of Morals*, academics wreak revenge by establishing a second-order monopoly that artificially restricts first-order trade by conjuring the spectre of 'Truth' (cf. 'God'), which is breached only at considerable, albeit vague, personal risk by the economically rational agent.

Even without succumbing to Nietzschean nihilism, we may identify two cross-cutting conceptions of rationality between which the state negotiates when making macroeconomic knowledge policy. Each conception starts with an agency – such as the university in the case of knowledge production – that perhaps historically emerged to mediate transaction costs between traders:

1 *Instrumental rationality*: The logic here is to analyse the several ends or functions the agency serves at once, disaggregating them to separate agencies that can each realize its specific end or serve its particular function more efficiently. Thus, over time, university's multiple services (e.g. teaching, research, community extension) may be better delivered by devolving its institutional structure into a cluster of discrete markets in which agencies compete to meet only one of the several demands that universities previously were expected to meet.

2 *Institutional rationality*: The logic here is to stress the optimality of the agency's handling of multiple ends or functions at once. Often this strategy is justified simply by noting that marketization carries its own costs, especially if the institution appears to be delivering its multiple services in a regular and prescribed fashion. In the case of universities, however, its unique institutional rationality also includes the synergy of its different functions, especially teaching and research, that would be lost if it were subsumed under the instrumentalist imperative.

The key point here is that the macroeconomic knowledge policymaker needs to *negotiate* between these two conceptions of rationality because each can be turned into self-serving rhetorics as specific parties try to gain an overall social and economic advantage, with instrumentalists focused on profits and institutionalists on rents (Fuller 2002: chap. 1).

While the transaction costs approach clearly cannot provide an adequate normative foundation for knowledge policy, it nevertheless uncannily captures the *empirical reality* of how much of knowledge policy is currently practised. Not only ordinary traders but also knowledge producers themselves may exhibit a 'need-to-know' attitude towards knowledge itself. Consider one of the most celebrated findings of information science, which has yet to be given its due by knowledge policymakers: *undiscovered public knowledge,* a concept introduced by University of Chicago librarian, Don Swanson (1986).

Swanson's starting point was the increasing amount of published research in all fields that goes unread and underutilized. Of course, part of this state of affairs is due to the sheer expansion of the number of researchers. But more disturbingly, most new recruits reinforce existing patterns of inquiry. In other words, even well-cited pieces of research tend to be cited for the same reasons. Add to that the number of pieces that are not cited – and probably not read – at all, and a strange epistemic purgatory results, one in which knowledge is produced without ever being fully consumed. Swanson showed that research from two quite different fields can be brought together to solve a standing problem in a third field. The problems which most concerned him were medical. In his original case, he successfully proposed fish oil as a remedy for the circulatory disorder, Raynaud's disease, based on observing (in the physiology literature) that the disease is characterized by high blood viscosity and (in the nutrition literature) that fish oil can reduce blood viscosity.

To be sure, Swanson had both the time and the interest to make the relevant cross-disciplinary connections – albeit *not* the expertise, as he was a physicist by training. Nevertheless, progress in one discipline was facilitated, if not revolutionized, by importing insights from other disciplines. If Swanson was able to do this thirty years ago, surely it should be easier to achieve today, given the advances in computerized search engines. What is needed, however, are incentives that encourage researchers to exploit the full range of undiscovered public knowledge before striking out on their own with a research funding proposal. Here, I will offer one such idea that could act as an incentive for interdisciplinary work more generally.

At the moment, the literature reviews in most grant applications are relatively perfunctory affairs, aimed at anticipatory appeasement of potential peer reviewers, who will then focus most of their assessment on the work proposed to be undertaken. However, it would be easy and beneficial to impose a higher standard on passing the literature review phase. This could begin simply by requiring the applicant to show whether other disciplines have (or have not) already dealt with the same or related problem, and then place a premium on showing that one would utilize work and perhaps personnel from other disciplines. Such a requirement could be economically justified as making the most of neglected knowledge, while avoiding diminishing returns on oversubscribed knowledge. In effect, the classically 'humanist' activity of reading and synthesizing other people's work seems to be required for science to live up to its own claims of efficiency as a mode of knowledge production!

However, universities and funding agencies need to reward researchers for proactively reading across disciplines to exploit undiscovered public knowledge. This is easier said than done. Perhaps the most fundamental problem here is that academia primarily rewards people for writing not reading – let alone reading across disciplinary boundaries. Moreover, the sort of reading that academic writing is supposed to reflect is not comprehensive but targeted to the intervention one already wishes to make in the research field. Put in the language of today's big data analysts, where the potential for underutilizing available data has grown exponentially, incentives are needed for academics to go beyond the mere 'data mining' of traditional search engines, which only reinforce the undiscovered public knowledge effect by delivering to the user what they are already looking for.

Instead, what is needed is outright 'data surfacing', which aims to 'emancipate' hidden data as program users are trained to see patterns characteristic of the data themselves, independent of any strategic goals or other preconceptions that users might have had for undertaking a search. This would entail a more exploratory search for patterns of ideas and findings which emerge from the entire body of academic literature, regardless of whether they track the preconceptions of discipline-based frameworks. In this, a cleverly designed computer-assisted form of interdisciplinarity could serve to undermine disciplinary path dependencies by regularly showing that reading across disciplinary boundaries is more productive than reading inside them. (Interestingly, the distinction between 'data mining' and 'data surfacing' turns out to be a coinage of the innovative Silicon Valley cybersecurity firm, Palantir.)

This current lack of incentive to probe undiscovered public knowledge reflects more than the usual tunnel vision associated with scientific training, which is then reinforced in the forums where specialists are required to subject themselves to periodic peer appraisal. More profoundly, it highlights the rather wishful attitude that scientists have towards the published record of their collective endeavours. (If epistemology captures how scientists know their objects of inquiry, I mean here *meta-epistemology*, i.e. the reflexive knowledge by which scientists come to know their own inquiries as a second-order object of knowledge.) They presume that any relevant insight would have already made its way to their publications, and more importantly, that it would have been followed up shortly after it was published. In this respect, the fact that the article Swanson uncovered had been ignored for several years was not a mark in its favour. It was presumed that the article was ignored for some good, albeit mysterious reason (i.e. involving an 'invisible hand' of some sort), not simply because it lay outside the given speciality.

The overall effect of these mental biases uncovered by Swanson is twofold. First, they serve to motivate endless calls for the funding of 'original research': findings absent from a discipline's short-term collective memory might as well have never been made. Second, such biases justify the use of relatively short (4–5–year) cycles to audit research performance: anything worth reading will have been read – and followed up – quickly, such that any article should be expected to enjoy a half-life approximating the length of the assessment cycle. Students of marketing will immediately recognize the pattern depicted here. Research has been made to conform to *fashion*, whereby both production and consumption patterns are subject to planned obsolescence (Fuller 2000a: chap. 5).

From a knowledge policy standpoint, we have here the flipside of innovation's valorization: *institutionalized amnesia* (Fuller 2006b: chap. 6). It would seem that a prime target of 'creative destruction' in intellectual innovation is the historical record itself. Those of a Machiavellian disposition might advise at this point that it would make sense to impose a statute of limitations on the criminality of plagiarism, such that plagiarism is punishable only if the works plagiarized were published within the current research assessment cycle. The benefits from earlier works will have already accrued to their authors, and if these benefits turn out to have been minimal, then they – and other authors – should have the opportunity to propose the same ideas as innovations in the next assessment cycle to see if they have better luck. Thus, what Swanson suggested already happens unwittingly would be licensed as a strategic course of action: namely, the *total* expiration of intellectual property rights over time – not only would inventors no longer receive royalties from users, but also authors would no longer be recognized for works they had produced.

In a knowledge management culture prone to model knowledge on the primary sector of the economy (i.e. as raw materials and natural resources, e.g. 'data mining'), this proposal may be best understood in the spirit of 'recycling', as opposed to simply 'wasting', unread texts (Fuller 2002: chap. 1). It may also help to reverse the systematic destruction of archives that even university libraries have justified on the basis of low levels of readership (King 2002). Perhaps, then, the stockpiling and classifying of books, journals and other information media would come to be undertaken with a metaphorical eye more to organ transplantation than embalmment. Indeed, this is one of the *better* outcomes likely to come from a knowledge regime that lacks a dedicated macroeconomic policy. Merton (1977) anticipated it as a corollary of the principle of cumulative advantage: to wit, obscure researchers interested in promoting certain ideas and findings should persuade better known colleagues to champion them under their own names.

3 WHY A MACROECONOMIC KNOWLEDGE POLICY VISION NEED NOT FAVOUR UNIVERSITIES

So far I have outlined the distinctive features of a macroeconomic knowledge policy perspective, as well as shown how even a microeconomic perspective as sophisticated as transaction cost analysis fails to provide an adequate basis for knowledge policy. But accepting the public good conception of knowledge promoted by the macroeconomic perspective does not necessarily imply that universities are the optimal delivery agents. However, the idea of public goods does presuppose a sensitivity to different time-frames within which the goods are delivered. The logic of university finance arguably fits this bill. Investment in higher education generates returns at various points over a long cycle, only some of which are realized in the short term by those who make the initial investments. The idea of the university as a 'creative destroyer of social capital' captures this idea (Fuller 2003): innovations that emerged from some unique configuration of interests are freely distributed through education, which often eventuates in the innovators losing their original market advantage. This practice has been historically justified by the use that students make of their training to further their own ends, which of course may also include the advancement of knowledge and general welfare.

Citizens have traditionally supported higher education through their taxes, even though few of them or their children have qualified for attendance. They have done so by virtue of the long-term benefits they believe they would receive from those who benefited from their taxes in the short term, namely, the funded matriculants who then went on to cure diseases or patent inventions that enhanced the general welfare. From that standpoint, the public finance of higher education may be seen as unleashing a Keynesian multiplier in the society at large, the full value of which can only be assessed in terms of the contribution that each individual makes to knowledge or welfare over a sufficiently long cycle and large scale. There are even multiplier effects from students who fail to produce socially beneficial knowledge, as they invariably consume resources along the way that serve to stimulate the local economy.

In this respect, Richard Florida's (2002) 'creative class' thesis can be seen as making macroeconomic knowledge policy the cornerstone of economic development more generally. According to Florida, a good state-based strategy for economic regeneration in a depressed region is to found a university, which will serve as a magnet for the high consumption of culture and connectivity, regardless of the university's quality or its denizens' long-term academic or economic success. Put a bit cynically, a college town is, from a macroeconomic perspective, a high-skill Vegas, a moment in the advance of 'casino capitalism' that its residents euphemistically call 'speculation'.

However, as we have seen, the 'long cycle' idea of macroeconomic knowledge policy is undermined by periodic assessment exercises for teaching and research, especially when these are evaluated separately: are the largest effects of research and teaching really felt within, say, four or five years? More generally, macroeconomic knowledge policy needs to navigate between too heavily *discounting the past* and *the future* (Fuller 2003). This is the Scylla and Charybdis of what might be called *inter-temporal management* – the system of intentions, expectations, outcomes and goals that lie at the heart of the policy process in its most general terms (cf. Elster 1983, Ainslie 1992). The two types of discounting arise when policymakers fail to adhere to a rigorous distinction between the means and the ends of policy, such that actual outcomes are presented as supporting the current policy. The past is discounted when actual outcomes are presented as sufficiently close to the original goals to be treated as equivalent (rather than a failure), while the future is discounted when the outcomes are presumed to be sufficiently indicative of those goals to warrant the policy's indefinite pursuit (rather than a change of course).

The Janus-faced nature of inter-temporal management of knowledge production recalls our earlier distinction between instrumental and institutional rationality. In terms of knowledge policy, the instrumentalist discounts the past, say, by allowing vocational training to pass for 'education', if graduation and employment rates rise to a policy-relevant threshold, whereas the institutionalist discounts the future, say, by promoting purely discipline-based research as 'potentially relevant', if it is produced at levels and publicized in channels that meet with policymakers' approval.

But behind this problem of rational inter-temporal management lies the deeper problem of the right frame of reference for making macroeconomic knowledge policy. A pioneering treatment of this topic with just the right mix of traditionalism and futurism is *The Uses of the University*, written by the first president of the consolidated University of California system, who coined the term 'multiversity' (Kerr 1963). There are at least four increasingly comprehensive sets of framing questions, starting with the presumptive centrality of the university to the production and distribution of knowledge and concluding with a perspective that divests the university of any special epistemic status:

1 Is each university a *sui generis* institution, as in the medieval sense of *universitas* (i.e. an autonomous corporation dedicated to the indefinite pursuit of ends that transcend the interests of the institution's current members)? In that case, each university needs to be judged on its own terms.

2 Does the term 'university' describe a higher-order category of institution within which exists considerable diversity yet all sharing some abstract overarching goals, e.g. the integration of teaching and research? In that case, there may be various dimensions along which all universities may be compared.

3 Is all of higher education best seen as part of a national education system that also includes primary and secondary education? In that case, are the aims of the three education sectors properly synchronized and the resources for achieving those aims properly allocated?

4 Is the education system itself perhaps best understood as a subsystem in a transnational knowledge economy? In that case, universities, as parts of this subsystem, should perhaps be judged in terms of their cost-effectiveness in the development of human capital. Other players here include think tanks and targeted vocational training programmes, not least those with relatively short traditions and based in virtual reality.

A macroeconomic knowledge policymaker ready to raise the fourth set of questions is effectively asking whether universities are indispensable to a comprehensive knowledge policy. Such *prima facie* scepticism attracts not only neo-liberals but also more welfarist reformers of institutional inertia. Either case reflects a tipping point whereby the rationality of institutions is judged by instrumentalist criteria, albeit the comprehensive ones of a macroeconomic policymaker. This is captured by the following menu of questions:

1 If you want to facilitate knowledge transfer, why have *any* institutional barriers between academia and non-academia?

   i Why not divest academics of any need to teach or publish? Should they not become more like the competition and hence be allowed to channel their activities into patenting and consulting?

   ii Why not use the inevitable departure of tenured faculty as an opportunity to turn university campuses into rental agencies whose tenants are hot-desking contract teachers and researchers, whose offices and equipment can be easily converted to conference facilities?

2 If you want to produce a flexible and adaptive labour force, why have *any* degree programmes that are unresponsive to market conditions?

   iii Why not convert all discipline-based units to temporary interdisciplinary ones that can be converted according to market demand, specifically as the expectations of prospective employers change?
   iv Why fetishize education as youthful front-loading, instead of encouraging many short courses periodically taken over the course of one's life?
   v Why allow universities to increase their student numbers, if the quality of instruction declines? Would it not be better to divert funds from universities to improve primary and secondary education? Such a strategy would both prevent a delay in job market entry and put a halt to credentials creep, whereby people tend to need more degrees to acquire comparable skills (Wolf 2002).

4 A CAUTIONARY TALE OF A PRO-UNIVERSITY MACROECONOMIC KNOWLEDGE POLICY: THE ALTHOFF SYSTEM

Given the above policy options, it would seem that the macroeconomic knowledge policymaker's horizon ultimately converges with that of the knowledge manager who, under the right conditions, is happy to eliminate universities as an efficiency saving. But this need not be the case. Let me conclude by offering a historical precedent for an alternative prospect, one that casts macroeconomic knowledge policymaking as a form of institutional entrepreneurship undertaken by the national education ministry. I refer to the case of Friedrich Althoff (1839–1908), who left a chair in economics at the University of Strasbourg to become higher education minister under Bismarck. Althoff succeeded in turning the recently united Germany into the world's premier scientific power in just one generation (1882–1907).

It has been generally acknowledged, from his contemporaries onwards, that the secret to Althoff's success lay in conceptualizing the knowledge sector as a multi-divisional business firm (*Wissenschaft als Grossbetrieb* in German) that fosters internal competition to meet common goals (Backhaus 1993). However, unlike the competition for resources associated with, say, the assessment of teaching and research at UK universities, Althoff did not strive to set targets or criteria independent of the field of play. Instead, he handicapped the field with an eye to achieving certain systemic ideals. Althoff clearly regarded 'university' as a unique institutional category that nevertheless can be subject to generic regulation, not simply the name shared by historically autonomous institutions with guild-like rights of self-governance. This difference of opinion distinguished

Althoff most sharply from Max Weber, who subjected Althoff's policies to critical scrutiny in the leading German newspapers (Shils 1974). For example, all candidates for professorial chairs were vetted through Althoff's office in Berlin, rather than left to local appointment committees. An accomplished academic himself, Althoff understood both the strengths and the weaknesses of the species. In particular, he used his far-flung networks to learn of emerging trends and stars whose promotion might both spark intellectual regeneration and inhibit local rent-seeking tendencies. Thus, Althoff typically refused to appoint a disciple of the retiring professor who would have then converted a field of inquiry into a fiefdom.

Weber was undoubtedly right that Althoff's policies had the long-term effect of shifting the balance of power over academic affairs in Germany from the universities to the state. Yet, Weber's moral indignation over this fact follows only if universities are indeed more reliable custodians of academic values than the state. In the case of Wilhelmine Germany, there was considerable room for doubt (Ringer 1969). Notwithstanding Weber's high-minded protestations, the guild-like character of German universities also made them bastions of prejudice – especially against Jews and women – that Althoff tried to correct. He was most successful in breaking down lingering regional barriers to German unification by hiring on what we would now call an 'affirmative action' basis that erased the difference between *de facto* Catholic and Protestant universities, in many cases by inserting Jews who excelled at the cutting edge of research. To be sure, it would be a mistake to cast Althoff's reforms entirely in the spirit of social justice. His primary concern was with forging a national academic identity, and like other nationalists he realized that the nation is strongest when all of its major social groups are represented in its flagship institutions, each trying to meet common goals in a competitive environment. 'Strength' here is to be measured mainly in Machiavellian terms as the power indirectly accrued to the state as the locus for resolving the countervailing forces of competing interests within its jurisdiction.

Althoff saw a special urgency in nationalizing (or, as Weber saw it, bureaucratizing) higher education because of its distinctive role in reproducing Germany's collective consciousness. When, at the start of the 19th century, Wilhelm von Humboldt turned the university into the vehicle of Enlightenment as we now know it (at least as an ideal), he was projecting a dynamic Germany always in the making that was to be forged more by language than by blood. What was striking then – and later to Althoff – was the very separation of language and blood. In this respect, like many other German intellectuals from Hegel to Weber, Althoff was fascinated by the precedent set by the United States, a country founded in the English language but with German blood (assuming a liberal view of German ethnicity – including the Nordic countries – and focusing on the period before 1900). This led him to foster academic exchanges with the US, the ironic benefits of which became clear after Germany's defeat in the 20th century's two world wars eased the transatlantic immigration of its scientists, resulting in English becoming the undisputed language of science (Gordin 2015).

However, at the time, Althoff believed that Germany's singular advantage over the US lay in its potential to merge academic and industrial interests in what, shortly after his death, were established as the Kaiser Wilhelm Gesellschaften (now called the Max Planck Institutes). Althoff presciently saw that in the 20th century the laboratory would come to replace the battlefield as the main theatre of war. The combination of capitalism's natural expansionism with science's tendencies to self-improvement and innovation thus seemed to be a smart strategy for alerting the world to Germany's ascendancy. Indeed, in the first half of the twentieth century, ambitious American scientific researchers regularly fled heavy college teaching loads for the freedom of industrial science parks, perhaps most notably Bell Labs in Murray Hill, New Jersey.

From a strictly organizational standpoint, Althoff pioneered the state-industry-academia 'triple helix' partnership that characterizes 'mode 2 knowledge production' today (Gibbons et al. 1994). He applied wholesale an industrial division of labour model to academia. Thus, preferential financial treatment was given to professors with a blueprint for managing a team of specialist researchers to achieve results on a scale unachievable by individual inquirers. (Kuhn's conception of 'paradigm' as disciplinary matrix was based on this image [Fuller 2000b: chap. 2].) However, the spirit of Althoff's institutional innovation could not have been more different from today's mode 2 knowledge production. Like most academics *circa* 1900, Althoff believed that science was reaching the end of its fundamental inquiries and hence ripe for application – what would be later called 'finalization' (Schaefer 1984) – with the national interest providing a covering theory, or ideology, and industry the material basis for its concerted extension. Given this vision, Althoff's version of the triple helix led to a marked expansion in the number of regular academic posts in order to embed the universities into the socio-economic infrastructure. In contrast, mode 2 knowledge production presupposes the postmodernist thesis that science has no intrinsic ends but is always open to multiple futures, especially now, given the relative decline of the nation-state *vis-à-vis* industry as an agent of science policy. Under the circumstances, universities are organized as fluid and adaptive structures staffed on an increasingly fixed-term basis.

Althoff demonstrated that macroeconomic knowledge policy could be made to great effect. While Weber may have been right that Althoff's idiosyncratic professorial appointments were not received well by local colleagues, they were nevertheless typically accommodated, since Althoff did not expect or encourage his appointments to abrogate the academic guild right to free inquiry. Moreover, Althoff's systematic disruption of intellectual dynasties, combined with a strong sense of the multiple sites of knowledge production and distribution, helped to wean German academics away from folding their distinctive insights into textbooks and handbooks that in the early years of the Second Reich had effectively converted every ambitious professor into a discipline onto himself (e.g. Wilhelm Wundt and experimental psychology). Althoff's unprecedented attempt to monitor the inputs and outputs of the higher education sector, with an eye to system optimality, presupposed that heretofore heterogeneous elements could be evaluated by a common standard – which in practice amounted to Althoff's own discretionary judgement: just as public and private sources of income could be aggregated, so too books and patents could be treated as equally valid knowledge products, each designed to have maximum impact over a specific time-frame and in certain sectors of the wider society.

Of course, the intellectual freedom promoted by Althoff came at a price, namely, an acceptance of the overriding primacy of the national interest. To be sure, scope was allowed for informed criticism of particular state policies, as Weber himself often made, especially when they appeared to contravene some overarching sense of the national interest. But in practice most academics were content to pursue politically uncontroversial lines of research with impunity. Yet, at the same time, the Althoff System was insensitive to the normative appropriateness of research relating to issues for which *institutional review boards* are now routinely convened. Institutional review boards are founded on the idea that the researcher's right to inquiry entails a reciprocal obligation to inform those participating in the research. Without such safeguards, research done in the national interest could well violate what we now regard as the 'human rights' of individuals or even entire groups.

This blindness was eventually turned to disastrous moral effect in the Nazi era, when medical researchers celebrated Hitler's staunch defence of free inquiry in the guise of minimal oversight in experiments involving human subjects (Deichmann 1996). One revealing moment was the Rockefeller Foundation's decision to pull its investments out of German physical science in the late 1930s because the physics community there seemed to be so clueless about the larger ambitions of the Nazi regime (Ball 2014). Indeed, the United Nations

Universal Declaration on Human Rights was partly motivated by the results of this sort of institutionalized blindness, which was a by-product of the Nazis having treated 'free inquiry' as an exclusively academic guild right (Weindling 2004). Nevertheless one might argue that in the wake of the Nuremberg Trials and alleged human rights violations associated with Cold War medical and psychological research the pendulum has now swung to the opposite extreme, whereby subjects are presumed to be in a *prima facie* adversarial relationship with scientists. In any case, this episode suggests that 'macroeconomic knowledge policy' needs to be applied more broadly across society – incorporating ideas of 'informed consent' in research – and not simply be limited to the academic sector, as the Althoff System did.

5 CONCLUSIONS AND THE KEY MACROECONOMIC CHALLENGE TO THE ACADEMIC CAESAR

The conclusion of most immediate relevance to today's 'audit culture' (Power 1997) – one which should focus the mind of any neo-liberal administrator – is the fundamentally misguided nature of microeconomic analyses of knowledge production that stress the need to show 'value for money' close to the point of service delivery. Such analyses do an injustice to the idea of knowledge as a public good. To be sure, just like private goods, public goods need to be manufactured and can be assessed in terms of costs and benefits. However, the spatial and temporal horizons required for an adequate assessment are much broader than for most private goods. In this context, it becomes important for the policymaker to 'see like a state' (Scott 1990). From that perspective, the university holds many attractions as an institution that is especially well designed to convert disparate discoveries in various fields into systematic knowledge that is regularly available, at least in principle, to the general population.

However, from the standpoint of general knowledge policy, it remains an open question whether self-governance is the best strategy to ensure the university's capacity to produce and distribute knowledge as a public good. This is the challenge which the neo-liberal administrator poses to the aspiring Academic Caesar. Perhaps a more systemic perspective is needed, the neo-liberal will argue. In the case of the Althoff System the full range of hopes and fears associated with a strong state-based macroeconomic knowledge policy were put on display. On the side of hope lies the system's capacity to make Germany the world's leading scientific power in less than a generation, while fostering a spirit of 'creative destruction' in an academic culture that had otherwise shown tendencies towards the maintenance of self-serving intellectual fiefdoms. On the side of fear, however, lies the ease with which German academia was allowed, even encouraged, to pool resources and orient research towards economic and political ends, which extended to a deep involvement in two disastrous world wars. Clark Kerr's (1963) 'multiversity', with its ultimate accountability to a democratically elected state legislature, may provide a model for reaping the benefits while avoiding the worst excesses of the Althoff System. In any case, the need for knowledge policy to be conducted at a macroeconomic level beyond that of the individual university is evident.

4

A VISION FOR THE FUTURE: THE PROACTIONARY UNIVERSITY AS A PLATFORM FOR THE ACADEMIC CAESAR

What follows is a vision for the university of tomorrow, one which takes forward the progressive features of the modern Humboldtian university, while regarding the institution itself as a whole greater than the sum of its academic and non-academic parts. However, in the future, what counts as human 'flourishing' will depend quite specifically on whether we treat *risk* as a threat or as an opportunity: that is, a *precautionary* or a *proactionary* attitude (Fuller and Lipinska 2014: chap. 1). The proactionary stance corresponds not only to the entrepreneurial spirit but also to Karl Popper's 'open society' and what Donald Campbell (1988) called the 'experimenting society'. It is a world in which people – in individual, collective and corporate form – are encouraged to conjecture boldly and to demonstrate their successes and make their mistakes in public, so that everyone might benefit. It is a world that aims to remove taboos and criminal sanctions from trying out radical new ideas, while at the same time recognizing that harms will be committed along the way, which in turn require recognition and compensation (Fuller and Lipinska 2014: chap. 4).

It is worth recalling that openness to risk has been a hallmark of modernity, which the Humboldtian university tried to underscore by exposing students to the cutting edge of research in their classroom experience – as opposed to their simply being taught the received wisdom. It was this general shift in approach that turned the university into a vehicle for 'Enlightenment' in the sense that Kant coined to capture his era. In this context, the Enlightenment may be seen as having embraced a 'symmetrical' approach to risk. On the one hand, the

past as a ground for authority was not nearly as secure as had been previously maintained; on the other hand, the future as a site for the realization of utopian dreams was not nearly as insecure. The former became the purview of the humanities, starting with the critical-historical approach to the Bible. The latter became the purview of the 'sciences', understood as those disciplines which took an experimental approach to data generation.

However, contemporary academia is biased against the proactionary and towards the precautionary on two political grounds, one relating to the decadent state of social democracy and the other to the power invested in institutional review boards.

By calling social democracy 'decadent', I mean that it is nowadays more concerned with protecting than empowering people. This point is very clear in Europe, where the precautionary principle is inscribed in European Union innovation-relevant legislation – resulting in, among other things, the public relations debacle surrounding 'genetically modified organisms'. Against this backdrop, neo-liberalism can seem like a breath of fresh air. Even though neo-liberalism fails to provide adequate recognition and compensation for failure, at least it removes paternalistic obstacles from the state, business and private individuals trying out new things. Moreover, because social democrats, like most of the political left nowadays, tends to focus on the losers (or 'vulnerable') in any political-economic regime, they can easily overlook the flexibility and adventurousness of neo-liberal regimes.

For a sense of what an empowering social democracy used to look like, consider that John Stuart Mill dedicated *On Liberty* to Humboldt – but the young Humboldt of *The Limits of State Action*, published in 1792, in the spirit of Kant and in the afterglow of the French Revolution – but twenty years before he became the academic supremo as we now remember him. In this context, Humboldt saw the universal task of education as the maturation of individual judgement, which in turn would result in the 'withering away of the state', as everyone could be trusted to make rational decisions on behalf of their own and the collective's interests. In such a world, direct democracy would reign supreme, and the state would be reduced to administering the decisions taken by this truly self-legislating polity. Of course, Marx later made this aspiration central to his Communist utopia, and Silicon Valley's fondness for tech-based replacements for state agencies may be read charitably as a 'post-educational' update of largely the same sentiment (cf. Morozov 2013). Put in terms of macroeconomic knowledge policy, Humboldt appeared to be calling for the state to plan for its own obsolescence by investing in an educational system specifically designed to wean people away from state paternalism. The proactionary university aims to rekindle just this spirit that seems to have been lost from the political left.

As for institutional review boards – the university committees which license academics to do research on living beings – in the previous chapter I characterized them as a precautionary overreaction to the Second World War experience. They end up instilling a needlessly adversarial relationship between science and the public. A potential research subject is configured as someone who might be personally abused (and hence safeguards must be in place to prevent that outcome) rather than as someone who might contribute to a larger human project. Of course, I do not deny the need for regulatory oversight on research, including the need for personal consent. But rather than pitting science against the public, science and the public should be joined in combat against some common enemy, be it defined as 'disease', 'death' or even 'extinction'. In this respect, institutional review boards might be usefully reworked as vehicles for brokering joint-stock companies formed by researchers and subjects for mutual benefit. And in terms of worst case scenarios from adventurous research, the legal orientation should be oriented more towards compensation than prohibition (Fuller and Lipinska 2014: chap. 4).

An Academic Caesar could even provide a stronger steer by dedicating an entire research programme or even institute to 'securitized risk-taking' as a general world-view, which should attract banks and insurance companies as potential funders. The point is to look at ways in which people have tried to build trust and achieve results in a highly volatile world – albeit not always with success. Consider, say, 'megaprojects', in which great achievements result from great faith combined with great underestimation of cost (Flyvberg et al. 2003). There could even be a national or even patriotic dimension in particular countries, such as the United States, whose history has been punctuated by this sort of self-understanding from its early colonial days to the era of space exploration.

On the teaching side, a liberal arts curriculum could focus on 'courage' as the operative virtue to which all incoming undergraduates would need to be exposed. This would not only provide historical and philosophical depth to entrepreneurship, but also would help academics to re-engage the military, whose existence, if acknowledged positively at all, has been honoured more in the breach than in the observance. Yet, the military has been more consistent than even business in fostering a 'strategic' mentality that plans for short-term setbacks and losses in service of long-term progress and victory (Tetlock and Gardner 2015: chap. 10). A courage-centred curriculum could be grounded in Plato's conception of *thymos*, a feature of the soul, dominant in the guardian class in the *Republic*, which regards creation and destruction as potentially of equal value *vis-à-vis* some overarching end. A subtle contemporary assessment of this virtue in the context of consumer capitalism is provided in Fukuyama (1992: chap. 17).

However, there is a deeper, more inbred resistance to proactionary thinking within academia. Throughout this book I have referred to it as *epistemic rent-seeking*. This is the tendency for disciplines to become increasingly proprietary in their relationship to organized inquiry. A discipline is 'proprietary' in this negative sense if it can compel inquirers to acknowledge its ownership of a field of inquiry, regardless of the disciplines' actual relevance to the epistemic ends of the inquirers in question. This 'rent' may take the form of requiring that the inquirers undergo specific discipline-based training or cite authors in the epistemic rentier's field. If organized inquiry is a kind of intellectual journey, then disciplines impose tolls along the way, perhaps for no reason other than having made a similar journey first. The extended critical discussion of peer review in this book may be read as addressing the various micro-level perversions of academic social relations that result from epistemic rent-seeking.

The natural opponent of the epistemic rent-seeker is what the sociologist Randall Collins (1979) has called the 'credential libertarian' who sees disciplinarians as George Bernard Shaw famously saw experts more generally, namely, as a conspiracy against the public interest. I am the rare academic who shares this point of view: appeal to expertise is the problem, not the solution, of humanity's epistemic predicament (Fuller 2002: chap. 3, Fuller 2015: chap. 5). The advent of the internet has launched a new and robust wave of credential libertarianism, as we are now always only a few keystrokes away from finding challenges and alternatives to expert opinion on virtually any topic. In this context, I have written of our entering a period of 'Protscience' on the model of the Protestant Reformation, whereby people take science into their own hands just as the early modern Christians took the Bible as a text which demanded a direct response from them (Fuller 2010a: chap. 4). The Academic Caesar would be foolish to underestimate Protscience's potential to erode the prerogatives of academic judgement. Thus, I argued early in this book that the university's best bet for retaining its epistemic authority in the future will be to function as the second-order regulator of all knowledge claims, regardless of who happens to make them.

The policy implication is that the Academic Caesar should refuse to take disciplinary boundaries, or any such purely academic identity markers, as sacrosanct. This is the only obvious way for the university to remain both strong and nimble in an increasingly competitive 'knowledge economy'. It is also the sense in which *interdisciplinarity* might be seen as an antidote to epistemic rent-seeking (cf. Fuller and Collier 2004: chap. 2). The 20th century's main science-based philosophical movement, logical positivism, plays a Janus-faced role in this strategy. On the one hand, it turned one discipline – physics – into the high-rent district of organized inquiry. On the other, the positivists demanded that other disciplines explain why they required theories and methods that differ from those of physics.

Logical positivism resembles the liberal imperialism promoted in Victorian Britain. Both were officially 'free trade' doctrines designed to promote relatively frictionless transactions in ideas and goods, respectively. But equally, both assumed a privileged position from which to espouse the free trade doctrine. In the case of the positivists, privilege was conferred on mathematics, be it symbolic logic or statistical representation.

The positivists expressed this line of thought as a distinction between the 'context of discovery' and the 'context of justification'. Science as an institution converts the idiosyncratic origins of discoveries into knowledge claims that anyone in principle can justify for themselves simply by examining the evidence and reasoning offered for a particular knowledge claim. In this way, individual insights come to be incorporated into a collective body of inquiry, which in turn empowers humanity as a whole. Thus, while a particular truth may have been discovered in a very particular way, the task of science is to show that it could have been uncovered under a variety of circumstances, provided the necessary evidence and reasoning.

It is easy to see how this positivist principle *could* sound the death knell to epistemic rent-seeking. The positivists themselves – much in the spirit of past imperialists and today's globalizationists – saw the removal of trade barriers as leading to greater integration and interdependency. Interdisciplinarity would be effectively fostered through a kind of anti-disciplinarity, at least insofar as disciplines would need to translate their specific jargons into a common lingua franca of intellectual exchange. Indeed, the positivists were early admirers of Esperanto, the would-be universal language promoted in the interwar years of the 20th century (Gordin 2015: chap. 5). Yet all did not go to plan. Just as in the economic case, the already existing power asymmetries between the disciplines played themselves out in this 'free trade zone'. While many disciplines became physics-friendly, non-physics-friendly modes of inquiry were consigned still further into the intellectual backwaters. Mathematics constituted a hidden barrier to free trade in this context.

Regardless of how the Academic Caesar resolves the problem of epistemic rent-seeking, the fact remains that academia trails behind 'Silicon Valley' in the consistent cultivation of a proactionary attitude towards risk. By 'Silicon Valley' I mean less the actual place than the global ideology that emanates from that part of the San Francisco Bay area. In this sense, 'Silicon Valley' is comparable to 'Manchester' in the early 19th century, as the name for a radical liberalism that created an alternative and durable knowledge base outside the university sector, centring on manufacturing and including a much wider range of people than universities had hitherto taken seriously. For their part, academics spent most of the 19th and the early 20th centuries playing catch-up by introducing science and technology-based education and research facilities into their campuses – as well as opening up their doors (somewhat more slowly) to the populace as a whole. Academia managed to evolve in the face of the 'Manchester' challenge and came out a stronger and more complex creature as a result. Indeed, Clark Kerr's (1963) 'multiversity' was an adaptation that has worked well for two generations. But the challenge is deeper now: 2016 is the new 1816.

Like the Manchester liberals, the Silicon Valley liberals are in their own high-tech way vulgar utilitarians, contemptuous of established institutions. However, they are not without ideas – and capital – to get things done, with or without universities. Academia needs to be more positive and creative in response to this development. A look at how it adapted to the original Industrial Revolution would not go amiss. Generally speaking, academia should not try to compete with the private sector in terms of capitalizing innovation. In this respect, I disagree with Daniel Greenberg (2007), the most venerable US critic of academic-state-industry relations, who would have universities claw back their intellectual property rights from industry. However, academia can play – and has played – a more substantial role than simply supplying relatively cheap intellectual labour for industry. Universities are where the 'normative horizons' of innovation are set, which means establishing standards of technical performance and cognitive frameworks that enable innovation to be understood systematically so that it can be taken to the next level. Moreover, all of this is streamed through a regularly revised curricular structure that allows people from all backgrounds to participate in the process. This is what I mean by calling for the university to be the producer of knowledge as a 'second-order good'.

In this context, an aim of general education must be to make people smarter than the environments in which they increasingly live and work. This standard will eventually serve to determine whether humans are needed at all – or, politely put, 'surplus to requirements'. Here I blame Steve Jobs, who created products with such 'smart' interfaces that they effectively dumbed down their billions of users by channelling their responses within an expected range, resulting in a second-order form of 'trained incapacity' that exceeds even the wildest fears of the phrase's originator, the early 20th-century US economist, Thorstein Veblen. Thus, even people who formally work in the 'IT sector' do not usually know that much about coding, algorithms, let alone the emerging political economy in which this new capital is being generated. Thus, alongside its classical goal of plugging students into established and 'classic' forms of academic knowledge, general education needs to address this very serious blind spot in contemporary culture. Rushkoff (2010) provides a call to arms, which hopefully will help raise the stakes in the need for 'digital literacy'.

The issue of general education raises the final point about the future of humanity, which returns me to the original theme of competing attitudes towards risk. In the last few years I have written of 'Humanity 2.0', which presumes that 'humanity', understood as an upgraded upright ape, has reached a crossroads in its development (Fuller 2011, 2012). It can identify with either (1) where we have come from (i.e. our status as one among many species on planet Earth) or (2) where we might go (i.e. the prospect of substantially altering if not abandoning those animal origins, including existing in some silicon form and/or in outer space). The former is what I call 'down-wing' and is associated with the precautionary principle; the latter 'up-wing' and associated with the proactionary principle (Fuller and Lipinska 2014: chap. 1).

I believe that this polarity will replace the existing right–left ideological polarity in the 21st century. The question then is how to teach it effectively. Here our species' relationship to the environment will provide a significant context. Will that relationship be defined as one of greater co-dependency with nature, *à la* down-wingers, even if that means scaling down humanity's reach over the planet? This has been the traditional stance of the ecology movement and certainly dominates contemporary discussions of global warming. Or, will our relationship be defined as one of greater 'decoupling', say, through the discovery of energy-dense materials (e.g. nuclear) that require much less biomass so as to enable us to continue progressing as we have? This is the way of the up-wingers, a notable case of which are the 'ecomodernists' (Nordhaus, Shellenberger et al. 2015).

REFERENCES

Abdool Karim, S.S., Bennett, N., Bergman, J., Clayden, P., Collins, S., Doms, R.W., Foley, B., Geffen, N., Hope, T., Kalichman, S., Koenig, S.P., Lederman, M.M., McCune, J., Moore, J., Nattrass, N., Smith, T., Stevenson, M., Wainberg, M., Weiss, R.A. and Witwer, K. (2009). 'Letter from US National Library of Medicine to MEDLINE concerning the de-selection of *Medical Hypotheses*', www.aidstruth.org/sites/aidstruth.org/files/NLMLetter-2009.08.05.pdf

Ainslie, G. (1992). *Picoeconomics*. Cambridge UK: Cambridge University Press.

Backhaus, J. (1993). 'The University as an Economic Institution: The Political Economy of the Althoff System'. *Journal of Economic Studies* 20 (4/5): 8–29.

Baehr, P. (2008). *Caesarism, Charisma and Fate: Historical Sources and Modern Resonances in the Work of Max Weber*. New Brunswick NJ: Transaction Books.

Ball, P. (2014). *Serving the Reich: The Struggle for the Soul of Physics under Hitler.* Chicago IL: University of Chicago Press.

Bell, A. (2012). 'Wider Open Spaces'. *Times Higher Education* (London) 19 April.

Benedetti, J. (2004). *Stanislavski: An Introduction*. London: Routledge.

Bloom, H. (1973). *The Anxiety of Influence.* Oxford: Oxford University Press.

Boden, R. and Epstein, D. (2011). 'A Flat Earth Society? Imagining Academic Freedom'. *The Sociological Review* 53: 476–95.

Bok, D. (1982). *Beyond the Ivory Tower*. Cambridge MA: Harvard University Press.

Bourdieu, P. (1990). *Homo Academicus*. (Orig. 1984). Cambridge UK: Polity.

Burawoy, M. (2005). 'For Public Sociology'. *American Sociological Review* 70 (February): 4–28.

Calhoun, C. (2006). 'Is the University in Crisis?' *Society* (May/June): 8–20.

Campbell, D. (1988). *Methodology and Epistemology for Social Science*. Chicago IL: University of Chicago Press.

Chandler, A. (1962). *Strategy and Structure*. Cambridge MA: Harvard University Press.

Clark, B. (1998). *Creating Entrepreneurial Universities: Organizational Pathways of Transformation.* Oxford: Pergamon-Elsevier Science.

Clark, W. (2006). *Academic Charisma and the Origins of the Research University.* Chicago IL: University of Chicago Press.

Clover, C. and Cookson, C. (2015). 'China Raises the Steaks in Cloning Research'. *Financial Times* (London) 24 November.

Cohen, I.B. (1985). *Revolutions in Science*. Cambridge MA: Harvard University Press.

Collins, R. (1979). *Credential Society*. New York: Academic Press.

Collins, R. (1998). *The Sociology of Philosophies: A Global Theory of Intellectual Change.* Cambridge MA: Harvard University Press.

Corbyn, Z. (2010). 'Unclear Outlook for Radical Journal as HIV/Aids Deniers Evoke Outrage'. *Times Higher Education* (London) 14 January.
Crow, M. and Dabars, W. (2015). *Designing the New American University*. Baltimore MD: Johns Hopkins University Press.
Deichmann, U. (1996). *Biologists under Hitler*. Cambridge MA: Harvard University Press.
Elster, J. (1983). *Sour Grapes: Studies in the Subversion of Rationality*. Cambridge UK: Cambridge University Press.
Florida, R. (2002). *The Rise of the Creative Class*. New York: Basic Books.
Flyvberg, B., Bruzelius, N. and Rothengatter, W. (2003). *Megaprojects and Risk: An Anatomy of Ambition*. Cambridge UK: Cambridge University Press.
Fukuyama, F. (1992). *The End of History and the Last Man*. New York: Free Press.
Fuller, S. (1988). *Social Epistemology*. Bloomington IN: Indiana University Press.
Fuller, S. (1996). 'Recent Work in Social Epistemology'. *American Philosophical Quarterly* 33: 149–66.
Fuller, S. (1997). *Science*. Milton Keynes UK: Open University Press.
Fuller, S. (2000a). *The Governance of Science*. Milton Keynes UK: Open University Press.
Fuller, S. (2000b). *Thomas Kuhn: A Philosophical History for Our Times*. Chicago IL: University of Chicago Press.
Fuller, S. (2001). 'A Critical Guide to Knowledge Society Newspeak: Or, How Not to Take the Great Leap Back to the Feudal Future'. *Current Sociology* 49(4): 177–201.
Fuller, S. (2002). *Knowledge Management Foundations*. Woburn MA: Butterworth-Heinemann.
Fuller, S. (2003). 'In Search of Vehicles for Knowledge Governance: On the Need for Institutions that Creatively Destroy Social Capital'. In N. Stehr (ed.), *The Governance of Knowledge* (pp. 41–76). New Brunswick NJ: Transaction Books.
Fuller, S. (2005). 'Social Epistemology: Preserving the Integrity of Knowledge about Knowledge'. In D. Rooney, G. Hearn and A. Ninan (eds.), *Handbook of the Knowledge Economy* (pp. 67–79). Cheltenham UK: Edward Elgar.
Fuller, S. (2006a). 'The Market: Source or Target of Morality?' in N. Stehr, C. Henning and B. Weiler (eds.), *The Moralization of the Market* (pp. 129–53). New Brunswick NJ: Transaction Books.
Fuller, S. (2006b). *The New Sociological Imagination*. London: Sage.
Fuller, S. (2006c). 'Universities and the Future of Knowledge Governance from the Standpoint of Social Epistemology'. In G. Neave (ed.), *Knowledge, Power and Dissent: Critical Perspectives on Higher Education and Research in Knowledge Society* (pp. 345–70). Paris: UNESCO.
Fuller, S. (2007a). *The Knowledge Book: Key Concepts in Philosophy, Culture and Society*. Durham UK: Acumen.
Fuller, S. (2007b). *New Frontiers in Science and Technology Studies*. Cambridge UK: Polity Press.
Fuller, S. (2009). *The Sociology of Intellectual Life: The Career of the Mind in and Around the Academy*. London: Sage.
Fuller, S. (2010a). *Science: The Art of Living*. Durham UK: Acumen.
Fuller, S. (2010b). 'Capitalism and Knowledge: The University between Commodification and Entrepreneurship'. In H. Radder (ed.), *The Commodification of Academic Research: Science and the Modern University* (pp. 277–306). Pittsburgh PA: University of Pittsburgh Press.

Fuller, S. (2011). *Humanity 2.0: What It Means to be Human Past, Present and Future.* London: Palgrave.
Fuller, S. (2012). *Preparing for Life in Humanity 2.0*. London: Palgrave.
Fuller, S. (2013a). 'On Commodification and the Progress of Knowledge: A Defence'. *Spontaneous Generations* 7 (1): 12–20.
Fuller, S. (2013b). 'Deviant Interdisciplinarity as Philosophical Practice: Prolegomena to Deep Intellectual History'. *Synthese* 190: 1899–1916.
Fuller, S. (2015). *Knowledge: The Philosophical Quest in History.* London: Routledge.
Fuller, S. and Collier, J. (2004). *Philosophy, Rhetoric and the End of Knowledge.* (Orig. by Fuller, 1993). Mahwah NJ: Lawrence Erlbaum Associates.
Fuller, S. and Lipinska, V. (2014). *The Proactionary Imperative: A Foundation for Transhumanism.* London: Palgrave.
Gibbon, E. (2000). *The History of the Decline and Fall of the Roman Empire.* (Orig. 1776). London: Penguin.
Gibbons, M., Limoges, C., Nowotny, H., Schwartzman, S., Scott, P. and Trow, M. (1994). *The New Production of Knowledge.* London: Sage.
Goffman, E. (1961). *Asylums*. Garden City NY: Doubleday.
Goodson, I. (1988). *The Making of Curriculum.* London: Falmer Press.
Gordin, M. (2015). *Scientific Babel: The Language of Science from the Fall of Latin to the Rise of English.* Chicago IL: University of Chicago Press.
Greenberg, D. (2007). *Science for Sale: The Perils, Delusions and Rewards of Campus Capitalism.* Chicago IL: University of Chicago Press.
Hacohen, M. (2000). *Karl Popper: The Formative Years 1902–1945*. Cambridge UK: Cambridge University Press.
Hofstadter, R. (1955). *The Age of Reform.* New York: Random House.
Humphreys, P. and Fetzer, J. (eds.) (1998). *The New Theory of Reference: Kripke, Marcus and Its Origins.* Dordrecht, Netherlands: Kluwer.
Javid, S. (2015). *Fulfilling Our Potential: Teaching Excellence, Social Mobility and Student Choice.* London: Department of Business, Innovation and Skills.
Kahneman, D. and Tversky, A. (1984). 'Choices, Values and Frames'. *American Psychologist* 39: 341–50.
Kerr, C. (1963). *The Uses of the University.* New York: Harper & Row.
King, R.G. (2002). 'Mad Archive Disease: Archival Spongiform Encephalopathy, the Loss of Corporate Memory, and the Death of Institutional Archives'. Paper delivered at the annual meeting of the combined Society of Southwest Archivists/Conference of Inter-Mountain Archivists, Flagstaff AZ (May).
Knorr-Cetina, K. (1999). *Epistemic Cultures: How the Sciences Make Knowledge.* Chicago IL: University of Chicago Press.
Kolowich, S. (2013). 'Why Professors at San Jose State Won't Use a Harvard Professor's MOOC'. *Chronicle of Higher Education* 2 January.
Kuhn, T.S. (1970). *The Structure of Scientific Revolutions* (2nd edn). (Orig. 1962). Chicago IL: University of Chicago Press.
Lamont, M. (2009). *How Professors Think: Inside the Curious World of Academic Judgement.* Cambridge MA: Harvard University Press.
Layard, R. (2005). *Happiness: Lessons from a New Science*. London: Penguin.
Lyotard, J.-F. (1983). *The Postmodern Condition.* (Orig. 1979). Minneapolis MN: University of Minnesota Press.

Marginson, S. (2007). 'The Public/Private Divide in Higher Education: A Global Revision'. *Higher Education* 53: 307–33.
May, R. (1997). 'The Scientific Wealth of Nations'. *Science* 275 (5301) (7 February): 793–6.
McGettigan, A. (2013). *The Great University Gamble.* London: Pluto.
McKenzie, R. and Tullock, G. (2012). *The New World of Economics* (6th edn). (Orig. 1975). Berlin: Springer.
Merton, R.K. (1977). *The Sociology of Science*. Chicago IL: University of Chicago Press.
Mirowski, P. (2002). *Machine Dreams: How Economics Became a Cyborg Science.* Cambridge UK: Cambridge University Press.
Mirowski, P. (2004). *The Effortless Economy of Science?* Durham NC: Duke University Press.
Mirowski, P. (2010). *Science-Mart: Privatizing American Science.* Cambridge, MA: Harvard University Press.
Mirowski, P. (2013). *Never Let a Serious Crisis Go to Waste: How Neoliberalism Survived the Financial Meltdown.* London: Verso.
Morozov, E. (2013). *To Save Everything, Click Here.* New York: Public Affairs.
Nordhaus, T., Shellenberger, M., et al. (2015). *The Ecomodernist Manifesto*. www.ecomodernism.org/
Nurse, P. (2015). *Ensuring a Successful UK Research Endeavour: A Review into UK Research Councils*. London: Department of Business, Innovation and Skills.
Popper, K. (1972). *Objective Knowledge*. Oxford: Oxford University Press.
Power, M. (1997). *The Audit Society*. Oxford: Oxford University Press.
Price, D. (1963). *Little Science, Big Science*. London: Penguin Press.
Proctor, R. (1991). *Value-Free Science? Purity and Power in Modern Knowledge.* Cambridge MA: Harvard University Press.
Quine, W.V.O. (1960). *Word and Object*. Cambridge MA: MIT Press.
Rescher, N. (2007). *Epistemetrics*. Cambridge UK: Cambridge University Press.
Ringer, F. (1969). *The Decline of the German Mandarins.* Cambridge MA: Harvard University Press.
Robbins, L. (ed.) (1963). *Higher Education: A Report of the Committee Appointed by the Prime Minister.* London: HMSO.
Roco, M.C. and Bainbridge, W.S. (eds.) (2002). *Converging Technologies for Improving Human Performance: Nanotechnology, Biotechnology, Information Technology, and Cognitive Science*. Arlington VA: NSF/DOC-sponsored report.
Rosen, R. (2012). 'Harvard Now Spending Nearly $3.75 Million on Academic Journal Bundles'. *The Atlantic* 23 May.
Ross, A. (ed.) (1996). *Science Wars*. Durham NC: Duke University Press.
Rothschild, E. (2001). *Economic Sentiments*. Cambridge MA: Harvard University Press.
Rushkoff, D. (2010). *Program or Be Programmed.* New York: OR Books.
Sandel, M. (2010). *Justice: What's the Right Thing to Do?* New York: Farrar, Strauss & Giroux.
Sassower, R. (2000). *A Sanctuary of their Own: Intellectual Refugees in the Academy.* Lanham MD: Rowman & Littlefield.
Schaefer, W. (ed.) (1984). *Finalization in Science*. Dordrecht, Netherlands: Kluwer.
Schumpeter, J. (1934). *The Theory of Economic Development*. Cambridge MA: Harvard University Press.

Schumpeter, J. (1942). *Capitalism, Socialism and Democracy*. New York: Harper & Row.
Scott, J.C. (1990). *Seeing Like a State*. New Haven CT: Yale University Press.
Seabright, P. (2004). *The Company of Strangers: A Natural History of Economic Life*. Princeton NJ: Princeton University Press.
Sharrock, W. (1974). 'On Owning Knowledge'. In R. Turner (ed.), *Ethnomethodology* (pp. 45–53). Harmondsworth UK: Penguin.
Shils, E. (ed.) (1974). *Max Weber on Universities: The Power of the State and the Dignity of the Academic Calling in Imperial Germany*. Chicago IL: University of Chicago Press.
Simon, H. (1977). *Sciences of the Artificial*. Cambridge MA: MIT Press.
Sohn-Rethel, A. (1978). *Intellectual and Manual Labour*. Atlantic Highlands NJ: Humanities Press.
Stewart, T. (1997). *Intellectual Capital: The New Wealth of Organizations*. London: Nicholas Brealey.
Swanson, D. (1986). 'Undiscovered Public Knowledge'. *Library Quarterly* 56 (2): 103–18.
Tetlock, P. and Gardner, D. (2015). *Superforecasting: The Art of Prediction*. New York: Random House.
Thaler, R. and Sunstein, C. (2008). *Nudge: Improving Decisions about Health, Wealth and Happiness*. New Haven CT: Yale University Press.
Turner, S. (2003). *Liberal Democracy 3.0*. London: Sage.
Wallas, G. (1914). *The Great Society*. New York: Macmillan.
Weber, M. (1958). 'Science as a Vocation'. In H. Gerth and C.W. Mills (eds.), *From Max Weber* (pp. 129–58). (Orig. 1918). Oxford: Oxford University Press.
Weindling, P.J. (2004). *Nazi Medicine and the Nuremberg Trials: From Medical Warcrimes to Informed Consent*. London: Palgrave Macmillan.
Westfall, R. (1980). *Never at Rest: A Biography of Isaac Newton*. Cambridge UK: Cambridge University Press.
Wilsdon, J. (2015). 'In Defence of the Research Excellence Framework'. *Guardian* (London) 27 July.
Winter, A. (2012). *Memory: Fragments of a Modern History*. Chicago IL: University of Chicago Press.
Wolf, A. (2002). *Does Education Matter? Myths about Education and Economic Growth*. London: Penguin Press.

INDEX